Implementing AI in Supply Chain Management

Introduction _____ 5

1. The Evolution of Supply Chain Management ___ 5

2. Understanding Artificial Intelligence in the Supply Chain _____ 13

Part 1: Preparing for AI Implementation _____ 23

3. Preparing for AI Implementation _____ 24

4. Building a Business Case for AI in Supply Chain 31

5. Selecting the Right AI Tools and Technologies _ 37

6. Organizational Readiness for AI _____ 45

Part 2: Core Applications of AI in Supply Chain _ 53

7. Demand Forecasting and Inventory Optimization _____ 54

8. Supply Chain Planning and Optimization _____ 61

9. Supplier Relationship Management with AI __ 67

10. Warehouse and Logistics Optimization _____ 75

11. AI in Procurement _____ 83

Part 3: Implementation Strategy — 92

12. AI Project Management Framework for Supply Chains — 93
13. Integrating AI with Existing Systems — 101
14. Managing Data for AI Success — 108
15. Scaling AI Solutions Across the Supply Chain — 115

Part 4: Challenges and Solutions — 122

16. Common Barriers to AI Adoption — 123
17. Overcoming Ethical and Compliance Concerns — 130
18. Dealing with Technological Challenges — 138

Part 5: Future Trends in AI-Driven Supply Chains — 147

19. The Role of IoT and Blockchain with AI — 148
20. Emerging AI Technologies for Supply Chain — 155
21. The Impact of Autonomous Systems — 163

22. Sustainability through AI in Supply Chain __ 172
23. Key Takeaways for Successful AI Implementation _____ 179
24. The Future of AI in Supply Chain Management _____ 186
25. Call to Action for Leaders and Practitioners 193

Introduction

1. The Evolution of Supply Chain Management

Traditional vs. Modern Approaches

The evolution of supply chain management is deeply rooted in the changing needs of businesses and the rapid technological advancements of the last century. Initially, supply chains were simple, linear, and predominantly localized. The processes revolved around basic procurement, manufacturing, and distribution functions with limited integration and coordination. Organizations often operated in silos, with procurement teams focused on sourcing raw materials, production teams managing factory outputs, and distribution teams ensuring delivery to customers.

Traditional supply chains were largely manual and heavily reliant on human decision-making. Operations were driven by experience, intuition, and basic historical data. Forecasting was rudimentary, involving manual records and spreadsheets, often leading to inaccuracies. Suppliers were chosen based on cost considerations, and relationships were transactional rather than strategic. Inventory management was conducted using fixed stock levels or reorder points, often resulting in either overstocking or understocking. Warehousing and logistics were labor-intensive, with little to no automation.

The limited communication and visibility across the supply chain posed significant challenges. Businesses lacked real-time insights, making it difficult to respond quickly to changes in demand, supply disruptions, or production delays. Lead times were long, and customer expectations were relatively low, with customers willing to tolerate delays. Efficiency was often sacrificed due to outdated processes, manual intervention, and an inability to collaborate across the supply chain ecosystem.

The transformation from traditional to modern supply chain management began with globalization and advancements in information technology. The interconnectedness of global markets placed new demands on supply chains, requiring businesses to focus on speed, flexibility, and cost-efficiency. The emergence of enterprise resource planning (ERP) systems in the 1990s was a game-changer, enabling organizations to integrate data across procurement, production, inventory, and distribution functions. ERP systems brought much-needed visibility, data centralization, and process standardization.

Modern supply chains are characterized by a shift from linear models to dynamic, interconnected ecosystems. The focus has expanded beyond efficiency and cost reduction to include agility, innovation, and customer-centricity. Companies today operate in complex global networks that involve multiple suppliers, contract manufacturers, logistics providers, and customers spread across geographical regions. As competition intensified, businesses began adopting lean and agile methodologies to optimize processes, minimize waste, and enhance responsiveness.

Technological advancements have also played a pivotal role in modernizing supply chains. The adoption of automation, robotics, and digital tools has enabled businesses to streamline processes, reduce human errors, and increase operational efficiency. Cloud computing has further accelerated this transformation, allowing organizations to store and analyze vast amounts of data while enabling real-time collaboration across global supply chain partners.

The shift toward customer-centric supply chains has fundamentally altered the way businesses operate. Customers today expect faster deliveries, personalized experiences, and higher product quality. This has forced companies to adopt demand-driven supply chain models that are powered by real-time data and predictive analytics. Organizations leverage data to gain actionable insights into customer preferences, demand patterns, and market trends, allowing them to optimize production, inventory, and distribution strategies.

Modern supply chains are also driven by sustainability and resilience. Businesses are under increasing pressure to reduce their environmental impact, improve resource efficiency, and ensure ethical sourcing. At the same time, disruptions caused by natural disasters, geopolitical events, and pandemics have highlighted the need for resilient supply chains that can withstand shocks and recover quickly. Organizations are now investing in risk management strategies, diversified supplier networks, and advanced planning tools to build more robust supply chains.

The Role of Technology in Transformation

Technology has been the single most significant driver of transformation in supply chain management. The adoption of digital tools, automation, and advanced technologies has enabled organizations to overcome the limitations of traditional supply chains and achieve higher levels of efficiency, visibility, and responsiveness.

One of the key technologies that has revolutionized supply chains is **data analytics**. Supply chains generate vast amounts of data from various sources, including procurement, production, inventory, and logistics. Advanced data analytics tools allow businesses to collect, process, and analyze this data to uncover patterns, identify opportunities, and make informed decisions. Predictive analytics enables organizations to forecast demand with greater accuracy, optimize inventory levels, and reduce the risk of stockouts or excess inventory.

The emergence of **artificial intelligence (AI)** and **machine learning (ML)** has taken supply chain optimization to the next level. AI algorithms can process vast amounts of data, identify trends, and make recommendations in real time. For example, AI-powered demand forecasting tools analyze historical data, market trends, and external factors to predict demand more accurately. Machine learning models continuously improve over time, allowing businesses to adapt to changing market conditions and customer preferences.

In warehouse operations, **automation** and **robotics** have transformed the way goods are stored, picked, packed, and shipped. Automated guided vehicles (AGVs), robotic arms, and autonomous mobile robots (AMRs) improve efficiency, reduce labor costs, and enhance order accuracy. Warehouse management systems (WMS) leverage AI to optimize storage space, streamline workflows, and ensure faster order fulfillment.

The Internet of Things (IoT) has brought unprecedented levels of visibility and control to supply chains. IoT-enabled sensors and devices are used to track goods, monitor equipment performance, and ensure product quality. For example, in transportation and logistics, IoT devices provide real-time tracking of shipments, enabling businesses to monitor delivery progress and address delays proactively. Sensors placed on manufacturing equipment allow companies to monitor machine health, predict maintenance needs, and minimize downtime.

The integration of **blockchain technology** has addressed some of the most pressing challenges in supply chain management, including transparency, traceability, and security. Blockchain enables businesses to create immutable records of transactions, ensuring that all stakeholders in the supply chain have access to accurate and reliable data. This is particularly beneficial for industries like food and pharmaceuticals, where product traceability is critical to ensuring safety and compliance. Blockchain also enhances trust among supply chain partners by providing a secure, tamper-proof record of transactions.

Another key technology driving supply chain transformation is **cloud computing**. Cloud-based platforms allow businesses to store and access data in real time, enabling seamless collaboration among global supply chain partners. Cloud solutions reduce the need for on-premises infrastructure, lower operational costs, and provide greater scalability. Organizations can leverage cloud-based ERP, WMS, and transportation management systems (TMS) to manage their supply chains more effectively.

The adoption of **digital twins** has further enhanced supply chain management by allowing businesses to create virtual replicas of their supply chain operations. Digital twins use real-time data to simulate and optimize processes, enabling organizations to test different scenarios, identify bottlenecks, and make data-driven decisions. For example, companies can use digital twins to simulate the impact of a supply disruption or assess the benefits of different inventory strategies.

In logistics and transportation, technologies like **route optimization software** and **autonomous vehicles** have revolutionized the way goods are delivered. Route optimization tools use AI to analyze traffic conditions, delivery schedules, and fuel efficiency to determine the most efficient delivery routes. Autonomous vehicles and drones are being tested and deployed to further reduce delivery times and costs.

The adoption of **augmented reality (AR)** and **virtual reality (VR)** in supply chain management has also gained traction. AR is used in warehouse operations to guide workers during picking and packing processes, reducing errors and improving productivity. VR is used for training and simulation, allowing supply chain professionals to develop skills and test solutions in a virtual environment.

The transformation of supply chain management is incomplete without mentioning the role of **cybersecurity**. As supply chains become increasingly digital and interconnected, the risk of cyberattacks has grown significantly. Organizations are investing in robust cybersecurity measures to protect their data, systems, and operations from threats. This includes implementing encryption, firewalls, and AI-driven threat detection tools to ensure the integrity and security of supply chain networks.

The convergence of these technologies has enabled businesses to transition from reactive to proactive supply chain management. Organizations can now anticipate disruptions, optimize processes, and respond to changes in real time. This level of agility and intelligence was unimaginable in traditional supply chains and has set new benchmarks for performance and customer satisfaction.

Modern supply chains are not just technology-driven but also data-driven. The ability to collect, analyze, and act on data has become a key differentiator for businesses. Companies that invest in digital transformation and embrace advanced technologies are better positioned to compete in today's dynamic and volatile markets. They can reduce costs, improve efficiency, and deliver superior value to customers, creating a significant competitive advantage.

The role of technology in supply chain management will continue to grow as businesses explore new innovations and capabilities. Emerging technologies such as quantum computing, generative AI, and autonomous systems promise to further disrupt and redefine supply chain operations. As supply chains become smarter, faster, and more resilient, businesses will be able to meet the demands of an increasingly globalized, digital, and customer-driven world.

The evolution of supply chain management has been a journey from fragmented, manual processes to integrated, technology-driven ecosystems. Businesses that embrace this transformation and invest in the right technologies will not only survive but thrive in the face of changing market dynamics. Technology is no longer a choice; it is a necessity for building supply chains that are agile, efficient, and resilient.

2. Understanding Artificial Intelligence in the Supply Chain

Artificial Intelligence (AI) is revolutionizing industries globally, and the supply chain sector is no exception. With advancements in AI, businesses are experiencing unprecedented improvements in efficiency, decision-making, and customer satisfaction. However, to fully leverage AI's capabilities, it is essential for supply chain professionals to understand the core aspects of AI, its applications, benefits, and the challenges companies face during its integration.

What is AI?

Artificial Intelligence refers to the simulation of human intelligence in machines that are programmed to think and act like humans. AI can be classified into narrow AI (or weak AI) and general AI (or strong AI). Narrow AI is designed to perform a specific task, such as recognizing speech or images, while general AI, which remains largely theoretical, would perform any intellectual task that a human being can do.

In supply chain management, AI is typically implemented as narrow AI. It performs tasks such as demand forecasting, predictive analytics, inventory optimization, and automated decision-making. The goal of AI in supply chain management is to increase operational efficiency, reduce costs, and improve responsiveness.

The rise of AI technologies stems from the increasing volume of data generated by supply chains. AI technologies, especially machine learning (ML), can analyze vast quantities of data far more efficiently than traditional methods. The ability to process and learn from data in real time is one of the core reasons AI has become such a game-changer in the supply chain domain.

Key AI Technologies for Supply Chains

The effectiveness of AI in supply chains is directly tied to its underlying technologies. These technologies enable supply chains to optimize operations, reduce inefficiencies, and achieve a level of automation that was previously unimaginable. The primary AI technologies transforming the supply chain include:

Machine Learning (ML)

Machine learning, a subset of AI, enables systems to learn from data and improve over time without being explicitly programmed. In the supply chain context, ML algorithms analyze historical data and identify patterns to make predictions and inform decision-making. This technology is extensively used in demand forecasting, predictive maintenance, and inventory management.

ML algorithms can forecast demand more accurately by learning from historical data, seasonal trends, customer purchasing behavior, and other external factors. These predictions enable businesses to make informed decisions regarding procurement, production schedules, and inventory levels, minimizing overstocking or stockouts.

ML is also used in predictive maintenance, where it analyzes equipment performance data to predict failures before they occur. By identifying patterns that indicate potential breakdowns, ML can help prevent downtime, improve equipment lifespan, and reduce maintenance costs.

Natural Language Processing (NLP)

Natural Language Processing (NLP) is another AI technology that allows machines to understand, interpret, and generate human language. NLP is used in the supply chain to process unstructured data like emails, invoices, customer feedback, and contracts. NLP can automate administrative tasks, improve communication, and help businesses gain insights from unstructured data sources.

One key application of NLP in supply chain management is chatbots or virtual assistants. These AI-driven tools can handle customer inquiries, track orders, and provide real-time updates, enhancing the customer experience. Additionally, NLP can extract key information from documents such as contracts or supplier performance reports, streamlining procurement and supplier management.

Internet of Things (IoT)

The Internet of Things (IoT) refers to a network of interconnected devices, sensors, and systems that communicate data to one another. In supply chains, IoT plays a critical role in providing real-time visibility into operations, such as tracking the movement of goods, monitoring inventory levels, and managing warehouse operations.

IoT devices can track the condition and location of goods in transit, allowing businesses to respond quickly to potential delays, disruptions, or spoilage. For instance, IoT sensors can monitor the temperature and humidity of perishable goods, ensuring they are transported under optimal conditions. This ability to track assets in real time ensures that businesses have the information they need to optimize routes, manage risks, and maintain high levels of service quality.

IoT can also integrate with AI systems to provide real-time data that enhances decision-making. For example, IoT sensors in warehouses can monitor stock levels and notify supply chain managers when it's time to reorder, preventing stockouts and minimizing excess inventory.

Robotic Process Automation (RPA)

Robotic Process Automation (RPA) uses software robots to automate repetitive, rule-based tasks in business processes. In the supply chain, RPA can handle activities such as invoice processing, order fulfillment, and tracking shipments. By automating these routine tasks, RPA reduces human error, accelerates workflows, and frees up human employees to focus on more complex tasks that require creativity and problem-solving.

For example, RPA can automate the reconciliation of purchase orders and invoices, ensuring that payments are processed promptly and accurately. In warehousing, RPA can help streamline inventory tracking, order picking, and shipping processes.

Predictive Analytics

Predictive analytics combines statistical analysis, machine learning, and data mining to forecast future trends based on historical data. In the supply chain, predictive analytics is used to forecast demand, predict supply chain disruptions, and optimize inventory. By analyzing historical data, predictive analytics can identify patterns and trends, helping businesses prepare for future events.

For instance, predictive analytics can forecast the demand for specific products, allowing companies to adjust inventory levels and production schedules accordingly. It can also predict supply chain risks, such as delays, disruptions, or price fluctuations, enabling businesses to proactively mitigate these risks and optimize their supply chain operations.

Benefits of AI Integration in Supply Chain

Integrating AI into supply chain management offers a host of benefits that help companies remain competitive in an increasingly globalized and dynamic market. Below are some of the key benefits:

1. Improved Efficiency and Productivity

AI-powered tools automate repetitive tasks, streamline operations, and optimize workflows, leading to greater efficiency and productivity. By reducing manual interventions, AI frees up time for employees to focus on more strategic tasks. AI can also identify inefficiencies in the supply chain and suggest improvements, which enhances operational performance across the entire supply chain.

For example, AI can optimize warehouse management by automating inventory tracking, reducing the time spent manually counting items, and ensuring accurate stock levels. Additionally, AI can optimize transportation routes in real-time, reducing travel time, fuel consumption, and operational costs.

2. Better Decision-Making

AI improves decision-making by providing data-driven insights that human decision-makers might miss. With AI, businesses can analyze vast amounts of data quickly, identifying patterns and trends that help make informed decisions. This is especially important in the supply chain, where decisions about inventory, procurement, production, and distribution can have a significant impact on costs and customer satisfaction.

For example, AI can analyze data on supplier performance, demand fluctuations, and market trends, helping businesses select the best suppliers and negotiate better contracts. It can also optimize inventory management, ensuring that businesses maintain the right stock levels to meet customer demand without incurring unnecessary carrying costs.

3. Enhanced Customer Experience

AI-driven supply chains are better equipped to meet customer expectations by offering faster delivery times, more personalized services, and real-time tracking. AI systems can predict customer demand, optimize delivery routes, and ensure that products are delivered on time. AI-powered chatbots and customer service tools can handle inquiries and complaints, providing immediate responses and resolving issues quickly.

For example, AI-driven recommendation engines can suggest products to customers based on their preferences and purchase history, leading to higher customer satisfaction and increased sales. AI can also enable businesses to offer faster and more accurate order fulfillment, ensuring that customers receive their products as expected.

4. Cost Reduction

AI helps supply chains reduce costs by automating tasks, optimizing processes, and improving resource utilization. AI-driven systems can optimize inventory levels, reducing excess stock and minimizing storage costs. It can also optimize transportation routes, reducing fuel consumption and delivery times.

Additionally, AI can predict supply chain disruptions and help businesses take proactive measures to mitigate risks. By reducing the risk of stockouts, overstocking, and other supply chain inefficiencies, AI contributes to cost savings and improved profitability.

5. Greater Flexibility and Agility

In today's fast-paced business environment, supply chains must be flexible and responsive to changing demand and market conditions. AI enables supply chains to adapt quickly by providing real-time data and predictive insights. AI systems can analyze data in real-time, identify potential disruptions, and suggest alternative solutions to keep operations running smoothly.

For example, AI can analyze weather patterns, market trends, and other external factors to predict demand fluctuations, allowing businesses to adjust production schedules or procurement strategies accordingly. AI can also identify potential supply chain risks, such as delays or quality issues, enabling businesses to take corrective actions before problems arise.

Challenges of AI Integration in Supply Chain

Despite the many benefits of AI integration, several challenges must be addressed for successful implementation. Some of the key challenges include:

1. Data Quality and Availability

AI systems rely heavily on high-quality, reliable data to produce accurate results. However, many businesses struggle with poor data quality, inconsistent data sources, and incomplete datasets. Without clean, structured data, AI systems cannot make accurate predictions or optimize processes effectively. Ensuring data quality and availability is essential for AI to function effectively.

2. Resistance to Change

Adopting AI in the supply chain often requires significant changes to existing processes and workflows. Resistance to change is a common challenge, as employees may fear that AI will replace their jobs or disrupt established workflows. Organizations must ensure that AI is introduced as a tool to complement human workers, not replace them. Training and upskilling employees are critical to overcoming resistance and ensuring a smooth transition to AI-powered processes.

3. Integration with Legacy Systems

Many supply chains still rely on legacy systems that are not compatible with modern AI technologies. Integrating AI with these systems can be complex and costly. Legacy systems may lack the data infrastructure necessary to support AI, making it difficult to implement AI-driven processes without significant upgrades.

4. Ethical and Regulatory Concerns

As AI becomes more integrated into supply chains, ethical and regulatory concerns will continue to arise. These concerns include data privacy, security, and transparency in AI decision-making. Organizations must ensure that their AI systems comply with relevant data protection laws and ethical standards.

Conclusion

AI is rapidly transforming the supply chain landscape, offering businesses unprecedented opportunities to improve efficiency, reduce costs, and enhance customer satisfaction. Understanding AI technologies and their applications is critical for supply chain professionals to harness their full potential. However, businesses must also address the challenges of data quality, resistance to change, integration with legacy systems, and ethical considerations to ensure successful AI adoption. As AI continues to evolve, supply chains that embrace these technologies will be better positioned to thrive in an increasingly complex and competitive global market

Part 1: Preparing for AI Implementation

3.Preparing for AI Implementation

Assessing the Current State of Your Supply Chain

Implementing Artificial Intelligence (AI) in the supply chain is not a one-size-fits-all solution. It requires a strategic approach that begins with a comprehensive assessment of the current state of your supply chain. This initial step lays the groundwork for identifying areas where AI can deliver maximum impact while minimizing potential disruptions. A clear understanding of the existing landscape helps organizations pinpoint inefficiencies, prioritize opportunities, and prepare for the complexities of AI integration.

Identifying Pain Points and Opportunities

The first step in assessing the supply chain involves identifying pain points that hinder operational efficiency, customer satisfaction, or overall business performance. Pain points can range from demand forecasting inaccuracies and inventory imbalances to supplier delays and insufficient visibility across the supply chain. Organizations must systematically evaluate each component of the supply chain—procurement, production, warehousing, logistics, and distribution—to uncover bottlenecks, inefficiencies, and recurring challenges.

For instance, if demand forecasting is frequently inaccurate, leading to overstock or stockouts, this becomes a prime candidate for AI-driven solutions like predictive analytics. Similarly, if supplier performance variability results in delays, AI tools can enhance supplier risk assessment and relationship management.

While identifying pain points is critical, organizations should simultaneously focus on uncovering opportunities for innovation and optimization. AI is not only a tool for addressing problems but also a means to unlock untapped potential. Opportunities may include automating routine processes, improving demand-supply alignment, enhancing customer service with intelligent chatbots, or reducing environmental impact through AI-enabled route optimization and waste reduction.

Collaboration among cross-functional teams is vital during this stage. Teams from procurement, operations, logistics, and IT should contribute their insights to ensure a holistic understanding of supply chain challenges and opportunities. Conducting workshops, surveys, and interviews can help gather valuable input from stakeholders and frontline employees who experience these challenges firsthand.

Data Readiness and Digital Maturity

The effectiveness of AI in supply chain management hinges on the availability, quality, and readiness of data. AI systems rely on vast amounts of data to generate insights, identify patterns, and make predictions. Therefore, assessing the organization's data readiness is a critical aspect of the preparation process.

Data Availability

The first question to address is whether the organization has access to sufficient data for AI to function effectively. Supply chains generate data at every stage—order histories, inventory levels, supplier performance metrics, transportation schedules, and customer feedback. However, this data often resides in silos across different systems, departments, or even partner organizations.

Organizations must ensure that data from disparate sources can be integrated into a centralized system for AI algorithms to process it comprehensively. Missing or fragmented data can limit the ability of AI tools to deliver actionable insights. Conducting a data audit is a useful approach to determine the availability and completeness of critical data.

Data Quality

Even if data is readily available, poor-quality data can undermine the success of AI initiatives. Data inaccuracies, inconsistencies, and duplications lead to flawed predictions and unreliable outcomes. Ensuring high-quality data requires robust data governance practices, including data cleansing, validation, and standardization.

For example, if transportation records are incomplete or contain errors, AI-driven logistics optimization tools will fail to provide accurate recommendations. Data quality issues are particularly common in organizations transitioning from manual processes to digital systems, emphasizing the need for rigorous data preparation.

Data Accessibility

Data accessibility is another crucial factor. Stakeholders across the supply chain must have seamless access to the data required for decision-making and AI application. This often involves breaking down organizational silos and implementing systems that promote data sharing and collaboration. Cloud-based platforms and supply chain control towers can facilitate real-time data access, improving AI's ability to generate timely insights.

Digital Maturity Assessment

AI implementation requires an underlying foundation of digital tools and technologies. Assessing the organization's digital maturity provides a clear picture of whether the supply chain is equipped to support AI initiatives.

Digital maturity refers to the extent to which an organization has adopted and integrated digital technologies into its operations. It encompasses infrastructure, systems, processes, and the workforce's ability to leverage digital tools effectively. Organizations with higher levels of digital maturity are better positioned to integrate AI seamlessly.

Key factors to consider in a digital maturity assessment include:

Existing Technology Infrastructure
Evaluate the current IT systems supporting supply chain operations. Are Enterprise Resource Planning (ERP), Warehouse Management Systems (WMS), and Transportation Management Systems (TMS) in place and functioning efficiently? Are these systems capable of integrating with AI solutions, or will they require upgrades?

Automation Levels
Determine the extent of automation in the supply chain. Highly manual processes may hinder AI adoption, as they lack the digital footprint required for AI tools to analyze and optimize operations.

Data Culture
Assess the organization's culture regarding data usage and decision-making. Is the workforce accustomed to leveraging data analytics, or are decisions primarily intuition-driven? AI thrives in environments where data-driven decision-making is a priority.

Technology Gaps
Identify gaps in the current technology stack that could impede AI implementation. For example, if the organization lacks IoT-enabled devices for real-time data collection, it may need to invest in sensors and connected devices before implementing AI-driven monitoring solutions.

Workforce Readiness

Digital maturity is not solely about technology; it also involves the workforce's readiness to adapt to AI-driven changes. This includes evaluating employees' technical skills, familiarity with digital tools, and openness to adopting new technologies. Resistance to change can pose significant barriers to AI adoption, making workforce readiness a critical consideration.

Developing a Roadmap

Once the current state of the supply chain has been assessed, organizations should develop a roadmap that outlines the steps needed to address gaps, capitalize on opportunities, and prepare for AI implementation. This roadmap should align with the organization's overall business strategy and include short-term, medium-term, and long-term goals.

For instance, the short-term focus may involve cleaning and integrating existing data, while medium-term goals could include piloting AI tools in specific areas such as demand forecasting. Long-term objectives might involve scaling AI solutions across the entire supply chain and integrating emerging technologies like blockchain or IoT.

The roadmap should also account for potential risks and challenges, such as the cost of technology upgrades, resistance from stakeholders, and the complexity of integrating AI with legacy systems. Building a robust change management strategy is essential to address these challenges proactively.

Conclusion

Assessing the current state of the supply chain is a foundational step in preparing for AI implementation. By identifying pain points and opportunities, ensuring data readiness, and evaluating digital maturity, organizations can establish a solid foundation for successful AI adoption. A thorough assessment not only clarifies the path forward but also enables organizations to prioritize investments and allocate resources effectively. As supply chains become increasingly complex and competitive, this preparatory phase is critical for unlocking the transformative potential of AI.

4. Building a Business Case for AI in Supply Chain

ROI Expectations and Metrics

Building a compelling business case for AI in the supply chain begins with a clear understanding of the return on investment (ROI). Stakeholders need to see tangible value, measured in terms of efficiency, cost savings, and enhanced customer satisfaction, before committing to significant financial and operational changes.

Defining ROI for AI in the Supply Chain

ROI for AI initiatives in the supply chain can be evaluated through direct and indirect benefits. **Direct benefits** include measurable cost reductions, such as lower transportation expenses through optimized routing or reduced inventory carrying costs due to improved demand forecasting. **Indirect benefits** may involve improved decision-making, better supply chain visibility, and enhanced agility in responding to market changes.

Organizations should adopt a structured approach to estimate the ROI of AI investments. This involves defining key performance indicators (KPIs) that align with strategic objectives and measuring the baseline performance of these KPIs prior to implementing AI. For example, if reducing stockouts is a priority, the baseline stockout rate should be established to assess the impact of AI-driven forecasting tools.

Key Metrics for Evaluating AI ROI

- **Operational Efficiency**: Metrics such as order cycle time, labor productivity, and inventory turnover rate can demonstrate how AI improves process efficiency. For instance, automated warehouse picking systems powered by AI can significantly boost order fulfillment rates.

- **Cost Savings**: AI solutions can reduce costs associated with logistics, procurement, and production. Metrics such as transportation cost per shipment, procurement cost per unit, and maintenance costs can highlight financial gains.
- **Revenue Growth**: Enhanced customer satisfaction and service levels resulting from AI applications can lead to increased sales. Metrics like on-time delivery rates and order accuracy are critical indicators of improved customer experience.
- **Risk Mitigation**: AI can reduce supply chain risks through predictive analytics, which anticipate disruptions and recommend contingency plans. Metrics such as supplier risk scores and disruption recovery time can help quantify risk reduction.

Examples of ROI in Action

- **Demand Forecasting**: AI-driven demand forecasting tools reduce forecasting errors, resulting in better inventory management. The ROI can be measured by reduced stockouts and excess inventory, as well as the associated cost savings.
- **Logistics Optimization**: AI-enabled route optimization reduces fuel consumption and delivery times. Metrics such as fuel cost savings and delivery time improvements provide tangible evidence of ROI.
- **Supplier Risk Assessment**: AI tools that analyze supplier performance and predict risks can prevent costly disruptions. The ROI is evident in terms of uninterrupted operations and avoided penalties due to missed deadlines.

Challenges in Calculating ROI

While calculating ROI is essential, it can be challenging to measure the full impact of AI initiatives, especially for indirect benefits like enhanced decision-making or long-term competitive advantage. Additionally, upfront costs for AI implementation, including software, infrastructure, and training, must be weighed against expected returns.

To overcome these challenges, organizations should adopt a phased implementation approach, starting with pilot projects that demonstrate quick wins and deliver measurable results. These pilots can serve as proof-of-concept initiatives to build confidence and refine the business case for broader AI adoption.

Aligning AI with Business Goals

A successful business case for AI in the supply chain is not just about ROI; it's about ensuring that AI initiatives are aligned with the organization's overarching business goals. Without alignment, even the most advanced AI solutions may fail to deliver meaningful value.

Understanding Strategic Priorities

Organizations must begin by identifying their strategic priorities and challenges. Is the focus on reducing costs, improving customer satisfaction, enhancing supply chain resilience, or achieving sustainability goals? AI initiatives should directly address these priorities. For example:

- **Cost Reduction**: AI-powered automation in warehouses can lower labor costs.
- **Customer Satisfaction**: Chatbots using natural language processing (NLP) can enhance customer service.
- **Resilience**: Predictive analytics can improve preparedness for supply chain disruptions.
- **Sustainability**: AI tools for route optimization can reduce carbon emissions.

By tying AI projects to specific goals, organizations can ensure that investments are justified and outcomes are relevant to their strategic direction.

Identifying Use Cases

Aligning AI with business goals requires identifying use cases where AI can make the most significant impact. Use cases should be evaluated based on their potential to address pain points, deliver measurable results, and align with organizational priorities.

For instance, if improving on-time delivery is a key goal, use cases such as predictive maintenance for transportation fleets or dynamic route optimization should be prioritized. Similarly, if cost reduction is a primary objective, use cases like spend analytics and procurement automation should take precedence.

Stakeholder Engagement

Building a business case for AI is not just a technical exercise; it's a strategic initiative that requires buy-in from stakeholders across the organization. Supply chain leaders, IT teams, finance departments, and executive leadership must collaborate to ensure alignment.

Engaging stakeholders involves:

- **Educating Teams**: Explaining how AI works, its potential benefits, and its alignment with business objectives.
- **Addressing Concerns**: Acknowledging potential challenges, such as job displacement or implementation risks, and proposing strategies to mitigate them.
- **Showcasing Benefits**: Presenting data-driven projections and pilot project results to build confidence in AI initiatives.

Cultural Alignment

Organizational culture plays a critical role in aligning AI with business goals. A culture that values innovation, data-driven decision-making, and cross-functional collaboration is more likely to embrace AI successfully. Leaders must foster a culture where employees understand the value of AI, feel empowered to contribute, and are encouraged to experiment with new technologies.

Roadmap for Implementation

Alignment also requires a clear roadmap that outlines how AI projects will be implemented, scaled, and integrated into existing operations. The roadmap should include timelines, resource requirements, and milestones to track progress.

Performance Monitoring and Continuous Improvement

Finally, aligning AI with business goals involves ongoing performance monitoring and refinement. Organizations should establish mechanisms to track the impact of AI initiatives on business objectives. Regular reviews and adjustments ensure that AI solutions remain aligned with evolving priorities and continue to deliver value.

Conclusion

Building a business case for AI in the supply chain requires a dual focus on ROI expectations and strategic alignment. By clearly defining ROI metrics, addressing challenges in measurement, and demonstrating tangible benefits, organizations can justify their investments in AI. Simultaneously, ensuring that AI initiatives are aligned with business goals guarantees that these investments drive meaningful outcomes and support long-term success. This approach positions organizations to harness the transformative power of AI and maintain a competitive edge in an increasingly complex and dynamic supply chain landscape.

5. Selecting the Right AI Tools and Technologies

Key AI Applications in Supply Chains

The selection of AI tools and technologies for supply chain management begins with understanding their diverse applications. Each application serves a distinct purpose, addressing specific challenges and unlocking efficiencies across various supply chain functions. Organizations must evaluate their unique needs to identify the most impactful AI applications that align with their operational objectives.

Demand Forecasting and Planning
AI-driven demand forecasting is one of the most transformative applications in supply chain management. By leveraging machine learning algorithms, companies can analyze historical sales data, market trends, and external factors to generate accurate demand predictions. AI tools in this area enable businesses to reduce stockouts, minimize excess inventory, and improve service levels. Real-time demand sensing further allows organizations to adjust production and distribution strategies dynamically in response to changing market conditions.

Inventory Optimization
AI technologies optimize inventory management by analyzing factors such as lead times, order frequencies, and customer demand patterns. Advanced tools can calculate optimal inventory levels, identify slow-moving or obsolete stock, and recommend replenishment strategies. This ensures a balance between meeting customer demand and minimizing carrying costs, ultimately improving cash flow and profitability.

Supplier Relationship Management
AI tools enhance supplier selection, performance evaluation, and risk assessment. Natural language processing (NLP) applications can analyze contracts and supplier

communications to identify potential risks, while predictive analytics flag suppliers prone to delays or quality issues. AI also facilitates automated supplier onboarding and communication, streamlining procurement processes and fostering stronger supplier relationships.

Logistics and Transportation Optimization

AI in logistics focuses on improving routing, scheduling, and overall transportation efficiency. Tools powered by machine learning and real-time data analytics help companies design optimal delivery routes, reducing fuel costs and transit times. Autonomous vehicles and drones are emerging as transformative solutions, enabled by AI for real-time navigation and decision-making.

Warehouse Automation

AI-powered warehouse technologies include robotic picking systems, automated storage solutions, and computer vision tools for inventory tracking. These technologies improve order accuracy, reduce labor costs, and accelerate fulfillment times. AI also assists in dynamic slotting, optimizing the placement of items within a warehouse to improve retrieval efficiency.

Fraud Detection and Risk Management

AI tools excel in identifying patterns of fraudulent activity across procurement, financial transactions, and supplier networks. Machine learning algorithms analyze vast datasets to detect anomalies, while predictive analytics helps organizations anticipate risks such as supply chain disruptions, geopolitical events, or natural disasters.

Quality Control and Production Optimization

AI technologies support predictive maintenance by analyzing equipment performance data to forecast potential failures. This minimizes downtime and ensures consistent production quality. Vision-based AI systems can also inspect products for defects, ensuring compliance with quality standards.

Customer Experience Enhancement

AI tools improve customer service by enabling personalized interactions, automated responses, and real-time updates. Chatbots and virtual assistants powered by NLP help resolve customer inquiries quickly, while predictive analytics ensures timely order fulfillment.

Sustainability Initiatives

AI tools contribute to sustainability by optimizing resource usage, reducing waste, and supporting eco-friendly supply chain practices. For example, AI-driven route optimization minimizes fuel consumption, while advanced analytics identify opportunities for recycling and reuse.

Choosing Between Off-the-Shelf Solutions and Custom Development

Once the key applications of AI are identified, organizations face a critical decision: whether to adopt off-the-shelf solutions or pursue custom development. Each approach has distinct advantages and challenges, and the choice depends on factors such as business requirements, budget, and technical expertise.

Off-the-Shelf Solutions

Advantages of Off-the-Shelf Solutions

Off-the-shelf AI tools are pre-built, ready-to-use software solutions designed for specific supply chain functions. Their primary advantage lies in their ease of deployment and cost-effectiveness. These solutions are typically developed by specialized technology providers, ensuring robust functionality and reliable performance.

Rapid Implementation

Off-the-shelf tools significantly reduce deployment timelines. Organizations can integrate these solutions into their existing systems with minimal customization, enabling them to achieve quick results.

Lower Upfront Costs
Compared to custom development, off-the-shelf solutions require lower initial investments. Businesses can avoid the costs associated with hiring development teams, acquiring infrastructure, and managing lengthy development cycles.

Proven Track Record
Commercial AI tools often come with case studies, user reviews, and industry validation, offering confidence in their capabilities. Vendors frequently provide customer support and regular updates, ensuring the tool remains up to date with evolving industry needs.

Challenges of Off-the-Shelf Solutions
While off-the-shelf tools offer convenience, they may lack the flexibility needed to address unique business requirements. Customization options are often limited, and organizations may need to adjust their processes to align with the tool's capabilities. Additionally, dependency on third-party vendors can lead to concerns regarding data security and long-term scalability.

Custom Development

Advantages of Custom Development
Custom AI solutions are designed specifically for an organization's needs, offering unparalleled flexibility and control. These tools can be tailored to address unique supply chain challenges, integrate seamlessly with existing systems, and evolve alongside the business.

Tailored Functionality
Custom-developed AI tools are built with the organization's specific processes, objectives, and pain points in mind. This

ensures a perfect fit, eliminating the compromises associated with off-the-shelf solutions.

Scalability and Adaptability

Custom solutions can be designed to accommodate future growth and changes in business requirements. Organizations can add new features, adapt to emerging technologies, and scale the solution as needed.

Competitive Advantage

By leveraging unique, proprietary AI solutions, businesses can gain a significant edge over competitors. Custom tools enable organizations to innovate and differentiate themselves in the market.

Challenges of Custom Development

Custom development requires substantial investments in terms of time, budget, and technical expertise. Building a solution from scratch involves extensive collaboration between supply chain professionals, AI experts, and software developers. The process can be resource-intensive, and the risk of delays or unforeseen challenges is higher than with off-the-shelf tools.

Decision-Making Criteria

Assessing Business Needs

The choice between off-the-shelf and custom AI solutions begins with a thorough assessment of business needs. Organizations should consider the complexity of their supply chain operations, the specific challenges they aim to address, and their long-term objectives.

For businesses with standard supply chain requirements, off-the-shelf solutions may suffice. However, companies operating in highly specialized industries or facing unique challenges may benefit from the flexibility of custom development.

Evaluating Budget and Resources
Budget constraints often influence the decision-making process. Off-the-shelf solutions are ideal for organizations seeking cost-effective, ready-to-use tools. Custom development, while more expensive, may deliver higher ROI in the long run for businesses with complex needs.

Considering Technical Expertise
The availability of in-house technical expertise is another critical factor. Organizations with robust IT and data science capabilities may find it easier to develop and maintain custom solutions. Conversely, businesses with limited technical resources may prefer the simplicity of off-the-shelf tools.

Scalability and Integration Requirements
Organizations must evaluate how well the chosen solution integrates with their existing systems, such as ERP, WMS, or TMS platforms. Custom solutions offer seamless integration and scalability but require careful planning. Off-the-shelf tools may require workarounds or third-party connectors to achieve compatibility.

Vendor Relationships and Support
For off-the-shelf solutions, the choice of vendor is critical. Organizations should assess the vendor's track record, support services, and commitment to innovation. Long-term vendor relationships are essential to ensure continuous improvement and alignment with evolving business needs.

Conclusion

Selecting the right AI tools and technologies for supply chain management is a strategic decision that impacts operational efficiency, customer satisfaction, and overall competitiveness.

By understanding the key applications of AI and carefully evaluating the trade-offs between off-the-shelf solutions and custom development, organizations can make informed choices that align with their objectives and resources. A structured approach to this decision-making process positions businesses to harness the transformative power of AI and unlock new opportunities for growth and resilience in an increasingly dynamic supply chain landscape.

6. Organizational Readiness for AI

Training and Upskilling Teams

The successful implementation of Artificial Intelligence (AI) in supply chain operations requires not just technological readiness but also human readiness. AI is not a standalone solution; its effectiveness depends on how well an organization prepares its workforce to adopt and use these tools. Training and upskilling teams is a fundamental component of organizational readiness, ensuring that employees possess the skills, knowledge, and mindset to leverage AI technologies effectively.

Understanding the AI Skills Gap

The rapid evolution of AI technologies has created a skills gap within organizations. Many employees in supply chain management have traditionally relied on manual processes, spreadsheets, and legacy systems. The transition to AI requires proficiency in new tools, data-driven decision-making, and analytics. This shift creates a need for targeted training programs that address both technical and non-technical competencies.

Key areas of the AI skills gap include:

- **Data Literacy:** Employees must understand how to interpret and use data effectively. AI systems rely on large volumes of data, and teams must know how to extract insights, validate results, and act on AI-driven recommendations.
- **AI and Analytics Proficiency:** Knowledge of machine learning algorithms, predictive analytics, and AI tools is critical for operational and managerial teams. While deep technical expertise may not be

required for all roles, a foundational understanding of AI processes is necessary.
- **Change Management Skills:** Adapting to AI solutions involves changing workflows, processes, and behaviors. Employees must be trained to manage change effectively, fostering flexibility and resilience in adopting new systems.

Designing Training and Development Programs

Training and upskilling initiatives must be tailored to meet the specific needs of various organizational roles. A comprehensive approach combines technical training, hands-on experience, and continuous learning opportunities.

Role-Based Training Programs
Different roles within the supply chain require varying levels of AI proficiency. For instance:

- **Supply Chain Leaders and Managers:** These professionals must focus on understanding the strategic applications of AI, interpreting AI-driven insights, and using them for decision-making. Training for leaders should emphasize ROI assessment, risk management, and business alignment.
- **Operational Teams:** Employees directly involved in day-to-day supply chain processes need training on using AI tools for tasks such as demand forecasting, inventory management, and logistics optimization.
- **Technical Teams:** IT and data teams require advanced technical training on AI systems, data engineering, and machine learning development to support implementation, integration, and maintenance.

Collaborating with External Experts
Given the complexity of AI, organizations may lack the in-house expertise needed to design and deliver training

programs. Partnering with AI specialists, academic institutions, or technology providers can help bridge the knowledge gap. Industry certifications, workshops, and courses offer employees access to cutting-edge AI concepts and practical applications.

Incorporating Hands-On Learning

Learning by doing is critical for building confidence and proficiency in AI tools. Organizations can implement pilot projects and simulation-based training where employees interact with AI systems in real-world scenarios. This hands-on approach helps teams understand how AI impacts workflows, improves problem-solving abilities, and reinforces their learning.

Promoting a Culture of Continuous Learning

The field of AI evolves rapidly, requiring organizations to foster a culture of continuous learning. Regular workshops, seminars, and online learning opportunities keep employees updated on the latest AI trends, tools, and applications. Providing access to digital learning platforms and incentivizing skill development encourages employees to stay engaged and proactive.

Measuring Training Effectiveness

Organizations must evaluate the success of their training initiatives to ensure readiness for AI implementation. Metrics such as knowledge retention, productivity improvements, and employee confidence in using AI tools provide valuable feedback. Surveys and performance assessments can identify further gaps and opportunities for improvement.

Cultural and Structural Changes Needed

Adopting AI in supply chain management is not just a technological transformation but also a cultural and structural shift. Organizations must cultivate a culture that embraces innovation, data-driven decision-making, and collaboration. Structural changes are equally important to align processes, roles, and hierarchies with the demands of AI-driven operations.

Fostering a Culture of Innovation

A culture of innovation is essential for AI implementation to succeed. Organizations must move away from traditional, siloed mindsets and encourage experimentation, creativity, and openness to change. Leaders play a critical role in setting the tone for innovation by communicating the value of AI and fostering a shared vision for its adoption.

Encouraging Data-Driven Decision-Making

AI thrives on data, and organizations must shift toward a data-driven culture where decisions are guided by insights rather than intuition. Employees at all levels must understand the importance of data accuracy, transparency, and collaboration. By prioritizing data-driven decision-making, organizations can maximize the value of AI tools and achieve measurable improvements in supply chain performance.

Breaking Down Organizational Silos

Traditional supply chains often operate in silos, with limited communication and coordination between departments such as procurement, inventory management, and logistics. AI requires seamless data sharing and integration across the entire supply chain ecosystem. Organizations must break down silos and promote cross-functional collaboration to ensure successful AI implementation.

Structural changes may include:

- **Cross-Functional Teams:** Establishing teams that bring together stakeholders from different supply chain

functions fosters collaboration and ensures AI solutions address end-to-end challenges.
- **Centralized Data Management:** Organizations must implement centralized data systems to provide a single source of truth for AI tools. This requires aligning IT infrastructure, processes, and governance across departments.
- **Redefining Roles and Responsibilities:** As AI automates routine tasks, employees' roles must evolve. Organizations must redefine job descriptions to focus on value-adding activities such as strategy development, decision-making, and relationship management.

Addressing Resistance to Change

Resistance to change is a common challenge when introducing AI into supply chain operations. Employees may fear job losses, struggle to adapt to new technologies, or feel uncertain about their ability to succeed in an AI-driven environment. Overcoming resistance requires transparent communication, leadership commitment, and employee engagement.

Communicating the Benefits of AI
Organizations must clearly articulate the benefits of AI implementation, emphasizing how these tools improve efficiency, reduce workloads, and create opportunities for professional growth. Leaders must address employee concerns openly, highlighting that AI is a tool for augmentation rather than replacement.

Involving Employees in the Process
Employees are more likely to embrace AI when they feel involved in the transformation process. Organizations should seek input from teams on pain points, challenges, and opportunities where AI can add value. Creating channels for feedback ensures that employees feel heard and valued.

Demonstrating Quick Wins
Implementing small, high-impact AI projects helps demonstrate tangible benefits and build trust among employees. Quick wins, such as improved demand forecasts or reduced lead times, showcase the value of AI and encourage broader acceptance.

Building Leadership Alignment

Leadership alignment is critical for driving cultural and structural changes. Executives and managers must champion AI adoption, ensuring alignment with organizational goals and long-term strategies. Leaders set the tone for AI readiness by modeling behavior, communicating expectations, and providing the necessary resources for success.

Providing Change Management Support
A structured change management framework helps organizations navigate the cultural and structural shifts required for AI implementation. Change management initiatives should include training, communication plans, and support systems to help employees adapt to new roles, processes, and tools.

Emphasizing Employee Development

AI adoption creates opportunities for employees to develop new skills and take on more strategic roles. Organizations must communicate this shift as a positive development, focusing on upskilling and career advancement opportunities. By investing in employee growth, organizations foster loyalty, engagement, and a sense of purpose.

The Role of Leadership in Shaping Readiness

Leadership plays a pivotal role in ensuring organizational readiness for AI. Leaders must balance the demands of technology adoption with the human aspects of change, guiding employees through uncertainty and empowering them to embrace AI-driven processes.

Creating a Shared Vision
Leaders must articulate a clear vision for how AI will transform supply chain operations and align with broader business goals. This vision should inspire confidence, providing employees with a roadmap for the future.

Leading by Example
Leadership teams must demonstrate their commitment to AI adoption by using AI tools, engaging in training programs, and embracing data-driven decision-making. Leading by example creates a culture of accountability and sets a positive precedent for employees.

Encouraging Innovation at All Levels
Innovation is not limited to senior leadership or technical teams. Leaders must create an environment where employees at all levels are encouraged to share ideas, experiment with new processes, and contribute to AI adoption. Recognizing and rewarding innovative thinking further reinforces this culture.

Organizational readiness for AI in supply chain management requires a balanced focus on training, cultural transformation, and structural alignment. By investing in upskilling initiatives, organizations empower employees to harness the potential of AI tools. Simultaneously, fostering a culture of innovation, collaboration, and data-driven decision-making ensures a smooth transition to AI-driven operations. Leadership commitment, transparency, and change management support are essential for overcoming resistance and driving success. A prepared workforce and adaptive organizational structure position companies to fully realize the transformative benefits of AI, unlocking new levels of efficiency, agility, and competitiveness in supply chain management.

Part 2: Core Applications of AI in Supply Chain

7. Demand Forecasting and Inventory Optimization

Predictive Analytics for Accurate Forecasts

Demand forecasting has always been a cornerstone of supply chain management, but traditional methods often fall short in managing the complexities of modern supply chains. Predictive analytics, powered by artificial intelligence, transforms the way organizations approach forecasting. By leveraging historical data, market trends, and external factors, predictive analytics enables businesses to achieve unparalleled accuracy in demand forecasts.

The Shift from Reactive to Proactive Forecasting

Traditional demand forecasting relies on historical sales data and rudimentary trend analysis. These methods often struggle to account for external variables such as weather patterns, geopolitical events, or sudden market shifts. Predictive analytics, enhanced by AI, shifts forecasting from reactive to proactive. AI models analyze vast datasets, identifying correlations and patterns that human analysts may overlook. This results in forecasts that are more dynamic and responsive to real-time changes.

How Predictive Analytics Works

AI-driven predictive analytics employs techniques such as machine learning, statistical modeling, and advanced data mining to generate accurate forecasts. The process typically involves:

- **Data Integration:** AI systems aggregate data from multiple sources, including point-of-sale systems, CRM platforms, social media, and market reports.
- **Pattern Recognition:** Machine learning algorithms detect patterns and relationships within the data, uncovering insights that inform demand trends.

- **Scenario Analysis:** Predictive models simulate various scenarios, allowing organizations to anticipate the impact of factors such as promotions, seasonality, or supply chain disruptions.
- **Real-Time Updates:** AI tools continuously refine forecasts as new data becomes available, ensuring they remain relevant and actionable.

Benefits of AI-Driven Demand Forecasting
The integration of AI in demand forecasting provides several strategic advantages:

- **Improved Accuracy:** By analyzing diverse datasets, AI reduces forecasting errors, enabling organizations to make more informed decisions.
- **Enhanced Agility:** AI models quickly adapt to changing market conditions, allowing businesses to respond proactively to demand fluctuations.
- **Optimized Resource Allocation:** Accurate forecasts enable efficient allocation of inventory, production capacity, and transportation resources, minimizing waste and costs.

Use Cases of Predictive Analytics in Demand Forecasting
Several industries have successfully adopted AI-driven demand forecasting to address specific challenges:

- **Retail:** AI helps retailers optimize stock levels, reducing overstock and stockouts while enhancing customer satisfaction.
- **Manufacturing:** Predictive analytics aligns production schedules with market demand, minimizing delays and excess inventory.
- **Healthcare:** AI models forecast demand for critical medical supplies, ensuring timely availability during emergencies.

Overcoming Challenges in Predictive Analytics Adoption

Despite its benefits, predictive analytics faces challenges in implementation. Organizations must ensure data quality, invest in robust AI tools, and train teams to interpret and act on AI-generated forecasts. Additionally, maintaining trust in AI requires transparency and validation of predictive models.

AI in Real-Time Inventory Management

Inventory management is a critical aspect of supply chain operations, directly impacting costs, customer satisfaction, and overall efficiency. Traditional inventory management systems rely on manual tracking and periodic reviews, often leading to inaccuracies and inefficiencies. AI-driven real-time inventory management offers a transformative solution by providing continuous visibility, automation, and optimization.

Real-Time Inventory Visibility

AI-powered systems provide organizations with end-to-end visibility of their inventory across multiple locations, including warehouses, distribution centers, and retail outlets. Using technologies such as IoT sensors, RFID tags, and computer vision, AI tools track inventory levels in real time, updating records automatically.

Advantages of Real-Time Visibility

- **Reduced Stockouts and Overstocking:** Real-time monitoring ensures optimal inventory levels, preventing costly stockouts or excessive inventory holding.
- **Improved Order Fulfillment:** With accurate inventory data, businesses can fulfill customer orders more efficiently, enhancing reliability and satisfaction.
- **Proactive Issue Resolution:** AI systems identify discrepancies or delays in inventory movement,

allowing organizations to address issues before they escalate.

Automation in Inventory Replenishment
AI enhances inventory replenishment processes by automating key decisions and actions. Predictive models analyze demand patterns, sales velocity, and supplier lead times to determine optimal reorder points. This automation eliminates guesswork, reduces manual effort, and minimizes errors.

Dynamic Safety Stock Management
Safety stock is essential to buffer against demand variability and supply chain disruptions. AI systems dynamically calculate safety stock levels based on real-time demand data, historical trends, and external factors. This approach ensures that safety stock is neither excessive nor insufficient, optimizing working capital.

AI-Driven Inventory Optimization
Optimization is at the heart of AI-enabled inventory management. Advanced algorithms identify inefficiencies in storage, transportation, and distribution, recommending adjustments to maximize resource utilization. Key areas of optimization include:

- **Warehouse Layout and Operations:** AI tools analyze picking patterns and storage requirements to optimize warehouse layouts, reducing travel time and operational costs.
- **Multi-Echelon Inventory Management:** For organizations with complex supply chains, AI optimizes inventory levels across multiple tiers, ensuring seamless coordination between suppliers, manufacturers, and distributors.
- **Sustainability:** AI-driven inventory optimization supports sustainability initiatives by minimizing waste, reducing emissions, and conserving resources.

Case Studies of Real-Time Inventory Management

Organizations across industries have achieved significant benefits by adopting AI-driven inventory solutions:

- **E-Commerce:** AI enables e-commerce companies to manage high-volume, fast-moving inventories efficiently, ensuring quick order processing and delivery.
- **Pharmaceuticals:** Real-time tracking of critical drugs and medical supplies improves patient care and compliance with regulatory requirements.
- **Automotive:** AI optimizes spare parts inventory, ensuring timely availability for maintenance and repairs.

Integration of AI with IoT for Inventory Management

The integration of AI with IoT devices enhances the capabilities of real-time inventory management systems. IoT sensors provide continuous data streams on inventory movement, condition, and location, while AI algorithms analyze this data to generate actionable insights. This combination creates a highly responsive and adaptive inventory management ecosystem.

Challenges in Real-Time Inventory Management

Implementing AI in inventory management comes with challenges such as:

- **Data Quality and Integration:** Ensuring accurate, consistent data across systems is critical for AI success.
- **Cost of Implementation:** Investing in AI tools, IoT devices, and infrastructure requires significant upfront costs.
- **Change Management:** Organizations must address resistance to change and provide training to ensure effective adoption.

Future Trends in AI for Inventory Management

As AI technologies continue to evolve, their applications in inventory management will expand. Emerging trends include:

- **Cognitive Automation:** AI systems will combine predictive analytics with prescriptive capabilities, autonomously executing decisions and actions.
- **Blockchain Integration:** Blockchain technology will enhance transparency and traceability in inventory management, improving accountability.
- **AI-Powered Sustainability Metrics:** Advanced algorithms will evaluate inventory practices against sustainability goals, enabling organizations to achieve greener supply chain operations.

Conclusion

Demand forecasting and inventory optimization represent core applications of AI in supply chain management, offering transformative benefits in accuracy, efficiency, and agility. Predictive analytics redefines demand forecasting by providing actionable insights and enabling proactive decision-making. Simultaneously, AI-driven real-time inventory management enhances visibility, automates replenishment, and optimizes operations, ensuring that organizations can meet customer expectations while minimizing costs and waste. By embracing these technologies, businesses can create more resilient and adaptive supply chains, positioning themselves for sustained success in an increasingly dynamic market environment.

8. Supply Chain Planning and Optimization

AI for Demand-Supply Matching

Demand-supply matching is one of the most complex yet critical functions in supply chain management. It ensures that production, procurement, and inventory levels align seamlessly with market demand while minimizing waste and maximizing profitability. Artificial intelligence has redefined the way organizations approach demand-supply matching by leveraging advanced data analytics, predictive modeling, and real-time insights to optimize supply chain decisions.

The Challenge of Balancing Demand and Supply
Traditional approaches to demand-supply matching often rely on static planning systems and historical data. These methods struggle to adapt to sudden shifts in demand, supply chain disruptions, or unexpected market conditions. In contrast, AI introduces dynamic capabilities, enabling supply chains to anticipate changes and respond proactively.

How AI Enhances Demand-Supply Matching
AI transforms demand-supply matching through the integration of real-time data, machine learning algorithms, and predictive analytics:

- **Real-Time Data Integration:** AI platforms collect and process data from diverse sources, including sales channels, production lines, and external market factors such as weather or geopolitical events.
- **Dynamic Forecasting:** Machine learning models analyze data patterns and trends to predict short-term and long-term demand fluctuations with high accuracy.
- **Optimized Allocation:** AI-driven optimization tools allocate resources, inventory, and production capacity efficiently, ensuring that supply aligns with projected demand.

AI Applications in Demand-Supply Matching

- **Dynamic Pricing Models:** AI adjusts pricing strategies based on demand elasticity and competitor behavior to manage demand more effectively.
- **Inventory Redistribution:** AI tools identify inventory imbalances across locations and recommend redistribution strategies to prevent overstocking or stockouts.
- **Supplier Collaboration:** AI systems facilitate better communication with suppliers by sharing demand forecasts and production plans, enhancing alignment and reducing lead times.

Benefits of AI in Demand-Supply Matching

- **Increased Agility:** AI enables supply chains to adapt quickly to changing demand and supply conditions, reducing delays and disruptions.
- **Cost Efficiency:** By optimizing resource allocation and reducing overproduction, AI minimizes waste and lowers operational costs.
- **Enhanced Customer Satisfaction:** Accurate demand-supply matching ensures timely product availability, improving service levels and customer loyalty.

Use Cases of AI in Demand-Supply Matching

1. **Retail:** AI-driven demand-supply matching helps retailers plan for seasonal spikes, promotions, and product launches, ensuring shelves are stocked appropriately.
2. **Manufacturing:** AI aligns production schedules with demand forecasts, reducing downtime and avoiding excess inventory buildup.

3. **Healthcare:** AI tools optimize the supply of critical medical equipment and pharmaceuticals, ensuring availability during emergencies.

Advanced Scenario Planning with AI

In today's unpredictable business environment, scenario planning is a vital tool for supply chain resilience. Advanced scenario planning enables organizations to evaluate potential outcomes of various decisions or external events, equipping them to prepare for uncertainties and mitigate risks. AI elevates scenario planning by enabling the creation of highly detailed, data-driven simulations and empowering decision-makers with actionable insights.

The Limitations of Traditional Scenario Planning

Traditional scenario planning often involves manual analyses and static models, which can be time-consuming and limited in scope. These methods may fail to capture the complexity of modern supply chains or account for real-time changes. AI overcomes these limitations by introducing speed, scalability, and precision.

How AI Transforms Scenario Planning

AI-powered scenario planning tools simulate multiple supply chain scenarios in real time, considering a wide range of variables, constraints, and interdependencies:

- **Predictive Modeling:** AI models forecast potential outcomes based on historical data, current trends, and hypothetical inputs.
- **Stress Testing:** AI systems simulate extreme conditions, such as supply chain disruptions, demand surges, or regulatory changes, to evaluate resilience and response strategies.
- **What-If Analysis:** AI tools enable decision-makers to explore various "what-if" scenarios, such as changes in

supplier availability, transportation delays, or raw material costs.

Key Components of AI-Driven Scenario Planning

1. **Data-Driven Insights:** AI integrates structured and unstructured data from internal and external sources to create comprehensive simulations.
2. **Interactive Dashboards:** Visual interfaces allow supply chain managers to adjust variables and view the impact of changes in real time.
3. **Automated Recommendations:** AI not only identifies potential risks but also suggests mitigation strategies based on scenario outcomes.

Benefits of AI in Advanced Scenario Planning

- **Proactive Risk Management:** By simulating potential disruptions, organizations can develop contingency plans and strengthen supply chain resilience.
- **Informed Decision-Making:** AI provides actionable insights that help businesses choose the most effective strategies for various scenarios.
- **Improved Resource Allocation:** Scenario planning ensures that resources are deployed efficiently, reducing costs and enhancing operational efficiency.

Real-World Applications of AI in Scenario Planning

- **Natural Disaster Preparedness:** AI helps supply chains simulate the impact of natural disasters, such as hurricanes or earthquakes, on logistics and inventory.
- **Regulatory Changes:** AI-driven simulations evaluate how new tariffs or trade restrictions could affect supply chain costs and routes.

- **Demand Volatility:** AI models predict the impact of demand surges during promotional events, holidays, or unforeseen market trends.

Challenges in Implementing AI for Scenario Planning

While AI brings significant advantages to scenario planning, it also presents challenges:

- **Data Quality and Availability:** Accurate scenario simulations require high-quality, comprehensive data.
- **Complexity of Models:** Building and maintaining AI models for scenario planning can be resource-intensive and technically demanding.
- **Organizational Buy-In:** Encouraging decision-makers to trust and adopt AI-driven insights may require cultural change and training.

The Future of AI in Scenario Planning

Emerging technologies, such as generative AI and quantum computing, are set to enhance scenario planning capabilities further. These innovations will enable supply chains to simulate even more complex scenarios and deliver near-instant results, paving the way for hyper-responsive and adaptive supply chain strategies.

Conclusion

AI has revolutionized supply chain planning and optimization by introducing sophisticated tools for demand-supply matching and advanced scenario planning. By leveraging predictive analytics, real-time insights, and dynamic simulations, organizations can achieve greater agility, efficiency, and resilience in their supply chains. As supply chain complexities grow, AI will continue to play a pivotal role in ensuring that businesses remain competitive and prepared for the challenges of tomorrow.

9.Supplier Relationship Management with AI

Supplier Selection and Risk Assessment

Effective supplier relationship management (SRM) is crucial for maintaining smooth operations, fostering innovation, and ensuring the resilience of the supply chain. Supplier selection and risk assessment are at the core of SRM, as choosing the right suppliers and evaluating the associated risks play a significant role in the long-term success of an organization. Traditional methods of supplier selection have typically involved manual processes, subjective evaluations, and a reliance on historical data, often leading to inefficiencies and inconsistencies. Artificial intelligence (AI) is transforming this space by automating key tasks, providing deeper insights into supplier performance, and enabling organizations to make more informed and data-driven decisions.

The Traditional Approach to Supplier Selection

In traditional supplier selection, businesses rely on a mix of qualitative and quantitative factors, such as price, delivery time, quality, and previous working experience. These decisions were often based on manually collected data and subjective judgment. While this approach has served companies well over time, it does not always offer a complete or accurate picture of a supplier's potential, especially when faced with global supply chains or rapidly changing market conditions.

How AI Enhances Supplier Selection

AI enhances the supplier selection process by enabling businesses to leverage vast amounts of structured and unstructured data to make more accurate and objective decisions. Machine learning algorithms analyze historical performance, market trends, and other relevant data to predict future supplier performance. These AI-driven tools can assess multiple criteria and weight them based on business priorities, ensuring that organizations select suppliers who best align with their operational needs.

AI-Driven Data Analysis for Supplier Selection

Machine learning (ML) models can analyze supplier data from a wide range of sources, such as past performance records, financial stability, customer reviews, and market trends. These algorithms can also integrate real-time data from suppliers' operations, such as lead times, inventory levels, and production capabilities. This holistic view enables companies to select suppliers who are not only cost-effective but also capable of meeting quality, delivery, and innovation standards.

AI-powered supplier selection platforms often include scoring systems that automatically rank suppliers based on predefined criteria. These systems can analyze both historical data and predictive factors to determine the likelihood that a supplier will meet future demand or address potential issues in the supply chain.

Risk Assessment in Supplier Relationships

The complexities of global supply chains expose organizations to various risks, including financial instability, political disruptions, quality issues, and natural disasters. Effective supplier risk management is therefore critical to minimize the impact of disruptions and maintain the continuity of operations. Traditional risk management strategies have often relied on basic supplier audits, manual assessments, and internal judgment, which can be inadequate for identifying emerging risks or mitigating long-term vulnerabilities.

The Role of AI in Risk Assessment

AI plays a vital role in improving risk assessment by enabling companies to predict potential risks before they materialize and take proactive measures to mitigate them. Machine learning algorithms are particularly effective at identifying hidden patterns and correlations within large datasets, allowing businesses to assess the risk profile of their suppliers more comprehensively.

Predictive Analytics for Risk Management

Predictive analytics, powered by AI, allows businesses to anticipate supplier risks based on historical data and current market trends. AI can analyze various factors, such as political instability, economic conditions, supplier financial health, and environmental risks, to provide a comprehensive risk assessment. By processing this information, AI can forecast potential disruptions, such as delays due to supplier bankruptcy or transportation bottlenecks, and help organizations prepare accordingly.

Real-Time Risk Monitoring

AI systems can continuously monitor suppliers and their operations in real time, using data feeds from various sources like financial reports, news articles, and social media updates. This real-time monitoring allows companies to stay ahead of potential risks by flagging suppliers who may be experiencing financial stress, labor issues, or other factors that could impact their ability to deliver goods or services. AI tools can also track changes in external factors, such as new regulatory requirements or geopolitical tensions, that could affect the supply chain.

Supplier Risk Scoring Models

AI-driven risk assessment tools often incorporate machine learning-based risk scoring models that assign a numerical risk value to each supplier based on various risk factors. These models can be customized to reflect the organization's specific risk tolerance, allowing businesses to prioritize their supplier relationships based on the level of risk they pose. For example, a supplier's financial instability may carry a higher risk score for an organization that depends heavily on timely payments, while a supplier's environmental risk may be more critical for a company focused on sustainability.

Automating Supplier Communication

Effective communication with suppliers is essential to maintaining strong relationships and ensuring the smooth flow of goods and services throughout the supply chain. However, manual communication processes, such as phone calls, emails, and traditional meetings, can be time-consuming and error-prone. Artificial intelligence is revolutionizing supplier communication by automating routine tasks, improving responsiveness, and ensuring more accurate and timely information exchanges.

The Importance of Timely and Transparent Communication

In supply chain management, information is key to success. Delays or inaccuracies in communication can result in disruptions, errors, or missed opportunities. Supplier communication needs to be transparent, fast, and efficient, particularly in industries with tight lead times or complex logistical networks. Automation powered by AI can facilitate this process by ensuring that the right information reaches the right people at the right time.

AI in Communication Channels

AI-based systems like chatbots and automated email responses are being integrated into supplier communication channels to streamline day-to-day interactions. Chatbots, for instance, can answer frequently asked questions, provide status updates, and resolve minor issues without human intervention. These AI-driven tools improve response times, reduce the workload of supply chain managers, and ensure that suppliers have immediate access to the information they need.

For example, AI-powered systems can automatically generate and send order confirmations, delivery status updates, and invoicing reminders to suppliers. By automating these routine tasks, companies can free up time for supply chain managers to focus on more strategic issues, such as negotiating terms or addressing supplier performance issues.

AI-Powered Communication Platforms

AI can also improve supplier communication through the integration of communication platforms with supply chain management systems. For instance, AI-driven platforms can automatically notify suppliers of any changes in order quantities, delivery schedules, or inventory needs, ensuring that suppliers are always up to date. These platforms can also facilitate collaboration by allowing suppliers to share real-time data on stock levels, production timelines, and other relevant metrics.

Natural Language Processing (NLP) for Supplier Interaction

Natural Language Processing (NLP) is another AI technology that enhances supplier communication by enabling more sophisticated and context-aware interactions. NLP allows machines to understand, interpret, and respond to human language, making it possible for supply chain systems to engage in more natural and personalized communication with suppliers.

For example, NLP-powered AI systems can read and interpret supplier emails, extracting key information such as order details, delivery dates, and payment terms. These systems can then generate appropriate responses or flag any issues that require further attention. NLP can also be used to analyze supplier feedback and sentiment, helping businesses understand the overall health of their supplier relationships.

The Benefits of Automating Supplier Communication

The automation of supplier communication brings several key benefits:

- **Increased Efficiency:** Routine tasks are completed faster, reducing the administrative burden on supply chain managers.
- **Improved Accuracy:** Automated systems reduce the risk of human error in communication, ensuring that all parties receive accurate and timely information.
- **Enhanced Supplier Relationships:** Faster and more transparent communication fosters stronger relationships with suppliers, improving collaboration and trust.
- **Cost Savings:** By automating communication, businesses can reduce the costs associated with manual processes, such as phone calls or staff hours spent on administrative tasks.

Challenges and Considerations

While AI offers significant benefits in supplier selection, risk assessment, and communication, it is essential for organizations to consider certain challenges when implementing these technologies. These include ensuring data accuracy and quality, maintaining supplier trust when using AI-driven systems, and overcoming resistance to change within the organization. Additionally, AI solutions must be carefully integrated with existing systems, such as Enterprise Resource Planning (ERP) and Customer Relationship Management (CRM) tools, to ensure seamless operation across the supply chain.

Conclusion

The integration of AI into Supplier Relationship Management is transforming the way businesses select suppliers, assess risks, and communicate with their partners. By leveraging predictive analytics, machine learning, and natural language processing, organizations can make more informed supplier selections, proactively manage risks, and automate routine communication tasks. As the complexity of global supply chains continues to grow, AI-powered SRM tools will be essential in helping businesses build stronger, more resilient supplier relationships and drive long-term success.

10. Warehouse and Logistics Optimization

AI-Powered Warehouse Automation

Warehouse operations are often among the most labor-intensive and complex aspects of the supply chain. Managing inventory, ensuring efficient product movement, and maintaining timely delivery schedules require meticulous planning and coordination. Traditional warehouse systems, while effective, are often challenged by the increasing demands of modern supply chains, especially as the complexity of product ranges and order volumes grow. Artificial Intelligence (AI) is revolutionizing warehouse operations by automating tasks, improving accuracy, and optimizing workflows, leading to enhanced efficiency and cost savings.

AI-powered warehouse automation combines advanced robotics, machine learning (ML), and data analytics to perform a wide range of tasks that were once manual or semi-automated. These systems enable warehouses to operate more efficiently, reduce human error, and meet the ever-increasing demands for faster delivery times and accuracy in order fulfillment.

Robotics and AI in Warehouse Operations

One of the key aspects of AI-powered warehouse automation is the use of robotics. Autonomous mobile robots (AMRs) and automated guided vehicles (AGVs) are increasingly being used in warehouses to transport goods, pick items from shelves, and move products across the warehouse floor. These robots are equipped with AI-driven navigation systems, enabling them to avoid obstacles, find the most efficient routes, and optimize their movements.

AI-driven robotic systems can improve inventory management by autonomously scanning shelves, counting stock, and identifying any discrepancies between physical stock and recorded inventory levels. This capability ensures that stockouts and overstocking are minimized, improving the overall accuracy of inventory records and reducing costs associated with inventory mismanagement.

AI-Driven Inventory Management

Inventory management is one of the most critical tasks in warehouse optimization, as it directly impacts product availability, fulfillment speed, and overall supply chain efficiency. AI can enhance inventory management by analyzing historical data, sales trends, and real-time information from other parts of the supply chain to predict demand and optimize stock levels.

Machine learning algorithms can forecast demand with high accuracy, allowing warehouses to maintain optimal stock levels and reduce excess inventory. By analyzing purchasing trends, weather patterns, seasonal demands, and other relevant data, AI can predict which products are likely to sell at a given time, allowing warehouses to stock the right amount of goods in anticipation of demand spikes. This results in more efficient use of storage space, better inventory turnover, and reduced waste from expired or obsolete goods.

Automated Sorting Systems

AI-powered sorting systems are transforming the way goods are organized and routed within the warehouse. Traditional sorting systems often require manual intervention, which can slow down the process and increase the risk of human error. In contrast, AI-powered sorting systems use machine learning to optimize the flow of goods through the warehouse.

These systems can automatically sort products based on various criteria such as size, weight, shipping destination, or priority level. By integrating with the warehouse management system (WMS), AI-powered sorting systems ensure that items are grouped efficiently and sent to the correct locations for further processing, reducing delays and improving overall throughput.

AI-Powered Quality Control

In addition to logistics and inventory management, AI is also making strides in quality control within warehouse environments. AI-driven visual inspection systems can automatically check for product defects, packaging errors, and damaged items. These systems use computer vision and machine learning algorithms to analyze product images and identify defects in real time.

AI quality control systems are more efficient than manual inspection processes, as they can work at much higher speeds and with greater consistency. This helps to maintain product quality standards while also minimizing the risk of human error. By detecting issues earlier in the process, AI can prevent defective products from reaching customers and reduce the need for costly returns.

Route Optimization and Delivery Scheduling

Efficient route planning and delivery scheduling are essential components of a well-functioning logistics network. As e-commerce has driven up the volume of small-package deliveries and customer expectations for faster delivery times, the need for optimized routing and scheduling has become more critical than ever. AI is playing a transformative role in this area, helping businesses to reduce transportation costs, improve delivery times, and enhance customer satisfaction.

The Role of AI in Route Optimization

Route optimization refers to the process of determining the most efficient routes for delivery vehicles to take, taking into account factors like distance, traffic, weather conditions, road closures, and delivery windows. Traditional route planning methods often rely on static data and limited decision-making criteria, which can lead to suboptimal results and increased costs.

AI-powered route optimization systems, on the other hand, use dynamic data and machine learning algorithms to continuously analyze and adjust routes based on real-time information. These systems can account for a wide range of variables, including current traffic conditions, driver behavior, delivery time windows, and even the availability of alternative routes. By analyzing vast amounts of data and considering all possible variables, AI can recommend the most efficient routes for drivers, minimizing delays and maximizing productivity.

AI in Dynamic Routing

Dynamic routing is one of the key advantages of AI-based route optimization. Unlike traditional systems that rely on pre-planned routes, dynamic routing continuously updates delivery routes based on real-time conditions. For example, if there is a sudden traffic jam or road closure, the AI system can automatically adjust the route in real time, ensuring that the driver takes the most efficient path available. This ability to adapt to changing conditions can save time, reduce fuel consumption, and help meet customer expectations for timely deliveries.

Predictive Analytics for Delivery Scheduling

AI can also be used to enhance delivery scheduling by analyzing historical data, customer preferences, and external factors like weather and traffic patterns. Predictive analytics allows companies to forecast delivery times with greater accuracy, helping them to optimize scheduling and improve on-time performance.

For instance, AI algorithms can predict the likely time of arrival for each delivery based on factors such as distance, traffic, weather, and driver history. By considering all these variables, businesses can offer customers more precise delivery time windows, which improves customer satisfaction and reduces the likelihood of failed deliveries.

Optimizing Fleet Management

Fleet management is another area where AI is making a significant impact. AI-powered fleet management systems can analyze vehicle performance, fuel usage, and maintenance schedules to ensure that vehicles are operating at optimal efficiency. Machine learning algorithms can also predict when a vehicle is likely to require maintenance, reducing downtime and extending the lifespan of the fleet.

In addition, AI can be used to monitor driver behavior, such as speed, braking patterns, and fuel consumption. By analyzing this data, companies can identify areas for improvement, implement targeted driver training programs, and ultimately reduce transportation costs.

AI in Last-Mile Delivery Optimization

Last-mile delivery—the final step in the delivery process—has become a major focus for optimization in modern logistics. It is often the most expensive and time-consuming part of the supply chain. AI can help optimize last-mile delivery by analyzing factors like customer preferences, delivery density, and vehicle availability to determine the best delivery method.

For instance, AI systems can determine whether a package should be delivered by a traditional truck, a smaller vehicle, or even through alternative methods like drones or autonomous vehicles. By optimizing the delivery method based on the characteristics of the delivery, businesses can reduce costs and improve delivery efficiency.

Improving Customer Experience through AI

Ultimately, both AI-powered warehouse automation and route optimization contribute to an enhanced customer experience. Faster processing times in the warehouse, coupled with optimized delivery routes, enable companies to meet customer expectations for faster and more reliable deliveries. AI-driven systems also enable better visibility into the supply chain, allowing customers to track their orders in real-time and receive updates on delivery status.

Challenges and Considerations in AI-Driven Optimization

While AI offers significant benefits in warehouse and logistics optimization, its implementation does come with challenges. These include the high upfront costs associated with AI technologies, the need for robust data infrastructure, and the requirement for ongoing monitoring and adjustments to optimize performance. Additionally, integrating AI solutions with legacy systems can sometimes be complex, requiring careful planning and collaboration between IT teams and operational staff.

Conclusion

AI-powered warehouse automation and route optimization are transforming the logistics and supply chain industries, providing significant benefits in terms of efficiency, cost savings, and customer satisfaction. By automating key tasks, optimizing inventory management, improving quality control, and enhancing route planning, organizations can achieve higher operational efficiency and stay competitive in a rapidly evolving market. However, the successful implementation of AI in these areas requires careful planning, investment in technology, and a commitment to continuous improvement.

11. AI in Procurement

The procurement function is undergoing a significant transformation with the integration of Artificial Intelligence (AI) technologies. AI provides procurement professionals with the tools to drive efficiency, optimize spending, manage supplier relationships, and reduce risks. By utilizing AI, procurement teams can analyze large datasets, automate repetitive tasks, and make more informed, data-driven decisions. The core applications of AI in procurement, including spend analysis, strategic sourcing, fraud detection, and contract management, are revolutionizing the way procurement teams operate and add value to their organizations.

Spend Analysis and Strategic Sourcing

AI-Driven Spend Analysis

Spend analysis is the process of collecting, cleansing, categorizing, and analyzing procurement data to identify spending patterns and opportunities for cost savings. AI enhances spend analysis by leveraging advanced machine learning algorithms and data analytics tools to process vast amounts of structured and unstructured data, allowing procurement teams to gain deeper insights into their organization's spending behavior.

AI-driven spend analysis tools can identify trends in supplier performance, spending distribution across categories, and potential inefficiencies. By analyzing historical purchase data, AI models can predict future spending patterns and provide recommendations for optimizing procurement strategies. These insights enable organizations to reduce costs by eliminating waste, identifying high-performing suppliers, and consolidating purchases where appropriate.

AI tools can also help procurement teams uncover hidden savings opportunities by identifying trends and inconsistencies in spending across different departments and business units. By standardizing and optimizing spending practices, organizations can improve cost management and ensure that procurement is aligned with the organization's financial goals.

Strategic Sourcing with AI

Strategic sourcing is a critical component of the procurement function, focused on identifying the best suppliers and negotiating contracts that deliver value for the organization. Traditional strategic sourcing relies heavily on human expertise and supplier relationships, but AI is now enabling procurement professionals to make more data-driven decisions.

AI-powered strategic sourcing platforms use machine learning algorithms to analyze supplier performance, financial stability, and other factors like delivery lead times, quality, and risk profiles. By processing large amounts of supplier data, AI can help procurement teams identify the most suitable suppliers for specific needs, enabling organizations to make better sourcing decisions.

AI-driven systems can also optimize the supplier selection process by analyzing supplier bids in real time. These systems use advanced algorithms to compare pricing, terms, and other factors to select the most favorable suppliers based on predefined criteria, such as cost, quality, and delivery performance. This reduces the time and effort required for supplier evaluation and ensures that organizations secure the best value in their sourcing decisions.

In addition, AI can assist with supplier segmentation by categorizing suppliers based on performance and risk. This allows procurement teams to focus on high-value suppliers while managing lower-risk suppliers more efficiently. Over time, AI can continuously refine its models to ensure that sourcing decisions remain aligned with business goals and market conditions.

Fraud Detection in Procurement

AI in Fraud Prevention

Fraud detection and prevention is an increasingly critical concern for procurement teams, as the risk of fraud, corruption, and other illicit activities continues to rise. Procurement fraud can take various forms, including overbilling, kickbacks, fake invoices, and fraudulent supplier relationships. AI technologies offer procurement professionals powerful tools to detect and prevent fraudulent activities before they escalate.

AI-based fraud detection systems leverage machine learning algorithms to identify anomalies in procurement data that may signal fraudulent behavior. These systems can analyze large datasets, including historical transactions, supplier information, and purchasing patterns, to identify patterns that deviate from the norm. For example, AI can flag suspicious transactions based on factors such as unusual spending patterns, recurring overpayments, or changes in supplier behavior.

By analyzing procurement data in real-time, AI systems can alert procurement teams to potential fraud as it occurs, enabling organizations to investigate and address suspicious activities quickly. Machine learning models improve over time as they learn from past instances of fraud, becoming more accurate in identifying emerging fraud schemes. These systems are also able to continuously monitor procurement activities, providing a level of vigilance that manual oversight alone cannot achieve.

AI in Risk Assessment

AI technologies are also highly effective in assessing supplier risk, which is a crucial aspect of fraud prevention. By evaluating various risk factors such as financial stability, regulatory compliance, and past performance, AI can help procurement teams identify high-risk suppliers that may pose a threat to the organization's integrity. These insights enable procurement professionals to proactively manage supplier relationships, ensuring that potential risks are mitigated before they become significant issues.

AI-driven risk assessment tools also allow for ongoing monitoring of suppliers. These tools can track financial health indicators, news about suppliers, and other risk factors in real time, providing procurement teams with up-to-date information on potential issues that could affect their relationships with suppliers. By identifying at-risk suppliers early, procurement teams can take steps to mitigate exposure to fraud and reduce the likelihood of supplier-related issues.

Contract Management with AI

AI-Powered Contract Creation and Analysis

Contract management is a critical aspect of procurement, as it ensures that agreements between buyers and suppliers are legally sound, cost-effective, and aligned with organizational objectives. AI is transforming the contract management process by automating key tasks, improving compliance, and reducing the risk of errors.

AI-based contract management systems can automate the creation of contracts by using natural language processing (NLP) and machine learning algorithms to generate standardized contract templates based on predefined rules and requirements. These systems can help procurement teams draft contracts faster and more accurately, ensuring that all necessary clauses are included and that the contracts are aligned with the organization's goals.

Moreover, AI systems can also assist in contract analysis by reviewing existing contracts and identifying key terms, obligations, and deadlines. Using NLP, AI can extract important information from contracts, such as payment terms, performance metrics, and penalties for non-compliance. This enables procurement teams to quickly assess the terms of a contract and ensure that all provisions are adhered to, reducing the risk of legal disputes or financial penalties.

Contract Compliance and Monitoring

Once contracts are in place, AI tools can help organizations monitor compliance throughout the contract lifecycle. AI-based systems can track key performance indicators (KPIs), such as delivery timelines, quality standards, and payment terms, to ensure that suppliers are meeting their obligations. By automating this monitoring process, procurement teams can identify issues earlier, leading to more effective contract enforcement.

Additionally, AI systems can alert procurement teams to potential risks, such as suppliers missing deadlines or failing to meet agreed-upon performance standards. By addressing these issues early in the process, organizations can avoid costly penalties and maintain strong supplier relationships.

Predictive Contract Management with AI

Predictive analytics is another powerful tool that AI brings to contract management. By analyzing historical data and trends, AI can help procurement teams predict the likelihood of certain events occurring during the contract lifecycle, such as late deliveries or contract breaches. This predictive capability enables procurement teams to take proactive measures to avoid potential issues, ensuring that contracts are executed smoothly and efficiently.

For example, AI-driven systems can analyze past supplier performance to predict the likelihood of a supplier meeting delivery deadlines in future contracts. If a supplier has a history of delays, the AI system may recommend alternative suppliers or contract clauses that provide additional safeguards to mitigate the risk.

Improved Decision-Making in Procurement

By leveraging AI in spend analysis, strategic sourcing, fraud detection, and contract management, procurement teams can make more informed, data-driven decisions. AI empowers procurement professionals to gain deeper insights into supplier performance, spending patterns, and contract compliance, which allows them to optimize procurement strategies, reduce risks, and achieve better value for the organization.

Furthermore, AI's ability to analyze vast amounts of data in real time enables procurement teams to make quicker decisions, reducing the time it takes to source products, evaluate suppliers, and execute contracts. This enhanced decision-making capability leads to more efficient procurement processes and better outcomes for the organization.

Conclusion

AI is transforming procurement by streamlining key processes such as spend analysis, strategic sourcing, fraud detection, and contract management. By leveraging AI tools, procurement teams can improve efficiency, enhance supplier relationships, and reduce risks associated with fraud and non-compliance.

As AI technologies continue to evolve, their applications in procurement will become even more sophisticated, enabling organizations to further optimize procurement strategies, drive cost savings, and achieve better results across the supply chain.

Part 3: Implementation Strategy

12. AI Project Management Framework for Supply Chains

Implementing AI in supply chain management is a complex, multi-faceted process that requires careful planning, execution, and continuous optimization. The AI project management framework for supply chains involves clear and systematic steps that guide the project from the initial planning phase through deployment and post-implementation evaluation. Whether an organization is implementing AI for demand forecasting, inventory optimization, procurement, or other supply chain functions, the project management framework ensures that all aspects of the AI deployment are aligned with business goals, technical requirements, and stakeholder expectations.

Key Steps from Planning to Deployment

Successful AI deployment in supply chains is driven by a well-structured project management process. Below are the essential steps to guide the AI implementation journey:

1. **Defining the Objectives and Scope** The first step in the AI implementation process is to clearly define the objectives and scope of the project. The organization must understand the problem it aims to solve with AI, whether it's improving demand forecasting accuracy, optimizing inventory management, or enhancing supplier selection. By aligning the AI project with specific business goals, the procurement and supply chain teams ensure that the AI solution will provide measurable value and address key pain points.

   The scope of the project should include identifying the specific processes and functions that AI will enhance. Defining the boundaries of the project, such as which supply chain functions will be automated and optimized, helps manage expectations and allocate resources effectively.

2. **Feasibility Assessment and Resource Allocation** Once the objectives and scope are defined, the next step is to conduct a feasibility assessment. This involves evaluating the technical and financial viability of the AI project. Feasibility studies assess factors such as data readiness, the complexity of existing systems, budget constraints, and the skill level of the internal team.

   Based on the feasibility study, the organization must allocate the necessary resources for the project. These resources include financial investments, technological infrastructure, and human capital, such as data scientists, supply chain experts, and AI consultants. Ensuring that the necessary resources are in place early on is crucial to the success of the AI deployment.

3. **Data Collection and Preparation** Data is the foundation of any AI project, and its quality directly impacts the effectiveness of AI algorithms. The data collection and preparation phase involves gathering historical supply chain data, cleaning and structuring the data, and ensuring that it is ready for analysis by AI systems.

   During this phase, organizations should also assess data privacy and security issues, ensuring compliance with relevant regulations. Proper data governance processes must be in place to maintain the integrity and confidentiality of data, especially when dealing with sensitive customer and supplier information.

4. **Developing the AI Model** After data preparation, the next step is to develop the AI model. This step typically involves working with data scientists and AI engineers to build, train, and test machine learning algorithms and models that will power the AI solution. Depending on the problem being solved, this could involve

supervised learning, unsupervised learning, reinforcement learning, or other machine learning techniques.

Developing a robust AI model requires continuous testing and fine-tuning. The model should be trained on historical data to identify patterns and insights that can inform supply chain decision-making. In many cases, iterative testing and model validation are required to improve the model's performance and accuracy before deployment.

5. **Pilot Testing and Validation** Before the full-scale deployment of the AI system, it is critical to conduct pilot testing. Pilot testing involves deploying the AI solution on a small scale within a controlled environment to evaluate its performance in real-world conditions. The pilot phase allows for testing the AI model against live data and assessing its ability to deliver the expected outcomes.

During the pilot phase, organizations should closely monitor key performance indicators (KPIs) to assess the success of the AI implementation. Pilot testing provides an opportunity to identify and address any issues that may arise before full-scale deployment. Feedback from key stakeholders, including supply chain managers and IT teams, can help refine the solution and improve its effectiveness.

6. **Full-Scale Deployment** After successful pilot testing, the AI solution can be deployed at full scale across the organization. Full-scale deployment requires the integration of AI with existing systems, such as enterprise resource planning (ERP) systems, warehouse management systems (WMS), and transportation management systems (TMS).

It is essential to ensure seamless integration during this phase to avoid disruptions in the supply chain. AI systems must be compatible with existing infrastructure, and proper data pipelines must be established to ensure real-time access to data. In many cases, organizations may need to work with vendors and consultants to ensure that the AI solution is fully integrated and operational.

7. **Post-Implementation Monitoring and Optimization** The deployment of AI does not mark the end of the project. Post-implementation monitoring and optimization are critical to ensuring that the AI solution continues to deliver value. During this phase, organizations should track the AI solution's performance against established KPIs and continuously assess its impact on business outcomes.

AI models may require periodic updates and re-training to ensure that they remain accurate and aligned with changing business needs. As new data is generated and supply chain dynamics evolve, AI models must be updated to reflect these changes. Continuous optimization ensures that the AI system remains effective in delivering insights and driving decision-making across the supply chain.

Agile vs. Traditional Approaches

When it comes to implementing AI in supply chain management, organizations must decide whether to adopt an agile or traditional approach to project management. Both approaches have their merits and can be applied depending on the specific requirements of the AI implementation project.

Traditional Approach

The traditional approach to AI project management follows a sequential, waterfall-style process, where each phase of the project is completed before moving on to the next. In a traditional project management model, the process typically follows a linear path, starting with extensive planning and progressing through design, development, testing, and deployment.

This approach is often suited for large-scale projects where the requirements are well-defined from the outset, and there is little likelihood of significant changes during the project lifecycle. It is particularly beneficial for organizations with clearly defined AI use cases and limited changes in scope during the implementation process.

However, the traditional approach can be more rigid and may result in delays or missed opportunities for optimization. If unforeseen challenges arise or if there are significant changes in the business environment, a traditional project management approach may struggle to adapt quickly.

Agile Approach

In contrast, the agile approach to AI project management is iterative and flexible. Agile methodologies involve breaking down the project into smaller, manageable segments, allowing teams to deliver value incrementally. Each iteration involves building and testing small components of the AI solution, with regular feedback from stakeholders.

The agile approach allows for more flexibility in adjusting the scope and direction of the project as it evolves. This is particularly useful in AI projects, where new insights and challenges may emerge during the development process. The iterative nature of agile allows for quick adjustments and continuous improvement based on real-time data and feedback.

Agile is ideal for AI projects that require rapid prototyping, frequent changes in requirements, and close collaboration between cross-functional teams. By prioritizing flexibility and continuous iteration, agile project management helps organizations stay responsive to market shifts and technological advancements.

Choosing Between Agile and Traditional Approaches

The choice between agile and traditional project management approaches depends on several factors, including the size and complexity of the AI project, the organization's culture, and the resources available. For AI implementations that involve a high degree of uncertainty or require continuous adaptation, an agile approach may be more suitable. However, for well-defined projects with clearly established goals, a traditional approach may be more effective.

Some organizations may also choose to combine both approaches, using agile methods for certain phases of the AI project (e.g., prototype development) while employing a traditional approach for others (e.g., full-scale deployment). This hybrid approach allows organizations to benefit from the strengths of both methodologies.

Conclusion

Implementing AI in supply chains requires a structured and methodical project management framework. From defining objectives and collecting data to deploying AI models and continuously optimizing the system, each step plays a crucial role in ensuring the success of the AI project. Whether adopting a traditional or agile approach, organizations must consider their specific needs, resources, and goals when choosing the most appropriate project management methodology. By following a clear, systematic approach to AI implementation, organizations can ensure that their AI solutions deliver meaningful value and drive improvements across the supply chain.

13. Integrating AI with Existing Systems

In today's fast-paced and increasingly digitalized business environment, supply chain organizations are leveraging Artificial Intelligence (AI) to enhance operational efficiency, reduce costs, and improve decision-making. However, integrating AI with existing systems such as Enterprise Resource Planning (ERP), Warehouse Management Systems (WMS), and Transportation Management Systems (TMS) is often a complex and challenging process. Ensuring that AI technologies are compatible with these systems and overcoming integration challenges is essential for realizing the full potential of AI in supply chain operations.

Compatibility with ERP, WMS, and TMS

AI implementation in supply chain management requires seamless interaction between multiple systems to ensure that real-time data is flowing between various touchpoints. In most organizations, ERP, WMS, and TMS are the core systems that manage critical supply chain functions. For AI to effectively enhance these functions, it must be integrated into these systems in a way that improves their performance while ensuring compatibility.

ERP Compatibility

Enterprise Resource Planning (ERP) systems are the backbone of many business processes, managing everything from procurement and inventory management to finance and human resources. Integrating AI with ERP systems enables organizations to automate and optimize various processes, such as demand forecasting, procurement decisions, and financial analysis.

One of the key challenges in integrating AI with ERP is ensuring that the data from multiple sources (e.g., sales, inventory, suppliers) is compatible with AI algorithms. AI systems require structured and high-quality data, often in real-time, to make accurate predictions and recommendations. Therefore, organizations need to ensure that the data stored in the ERP system is clean, accurate, and accessible to AI models.

AI can significantly enhance ERP systems by enabling features such as intelligent data processing, predictive analytics, and automation of routine tasks. For example, AI-powered forecasting models can use historical sales data to predict future demand, helping supply chain managers optimize stock levels and reduce waste. Additionally, AI can assist in streamlining procurement workflows, automating purchase orders based on predicted demand and supplier performance.

To achieve effective integration, ERP vendors must be open to adopting AI functionalities, and organizations may need to customize their ERP systems or choose specialized AI integration tools that can work with the ERP system's existing architecture.

WMS Compatibility

Warehouse Management Systems (WMS) help companies manage warehouse operations, including inventory tracking, order fulfillment, and shipment planning. Integrating AI into WMS offers significant benefits, such as optimizing warehouse layouts, improving order picking accuracy, and enhancing inventory management.

AI can provide predictive insights that help improve decision-making within the WMS, such as recommending the best storage locations for products based on predicted demand or optimizing inventory levels to reduce stockouts or overstocking. Additionally, AI-powered robotics and automation can further enhance warehouse operations by automating tasks like sorting, picking, and packing.

However, integrating AI with WMS presents challenges. WMS systems often rely on a predefined set of workflows and processes, which can be difficult to modify to accommodate AI-driven capabilities. Organizations must ensure that their AI solutions are flexible enough to work with existing WMS configurations while providing additional value.

The integration process involves aligning AI models with existing warehouse operations and data flows, ensuring that AI algorithms receive up-to-date and accurate information about inventory, order status, and product movement. Moreover, organizations may need to invest in additional hardware, such as sensors, cameras, and automated vehicles, to fully capitalize on AI capabilities within the warehouse.

TMS Compatibility

Transportation Management Systems (TMS) are essential for optimizing the movement of goods, including route planning, carrier selection, and freight management. By integrating AI into TMS, organizations can enhance the efficiency of their transportation operations, reduce costs, and improve delivery performance.

AI in TMS can assist in route optimization by considering multiple variables, such as traffic patterns, weather conditions, and delivery time windows, to recommend the most efficient routes. Additionally, AI can predict potential disruptions in the supply chain (e.g., delays due to weather or traffic) and suggest alternative routes or solutions to minimize delays.

The challenge in integrating AI with TMS lies in aligning AI algorithms with the complexities of transportation networks. AI models must process vast amounts of data from different sources, such as GPS data, traffic reports, and weather forecasts, to generate actionable insights. Integrating these sources of data with the TMS system requires robust APIs and data pipelines to ensure that the AI algorithms receive real-time data for optimal decision-making.

Overcoming Integration Challenges

Despite the significant benefits of integrating AI with existing systems, several challenges can arise during the integration process. Overcoming these challenges requires careful planning, the right technical expertise, and strategic alignment between IT and business teams.

Data Quality and Compatibility

AI models are only as effective as the data they process. Poor data quality or incompatible data formats can significantly undermine the performance of AI systems. Integrating AI into existing supply chain systems requires a focus on data quality and ensuring that data from ERP, WMS, and TMS systems is clean, accurate, and structured in a way that can be easily ingested by AI models.

Data from different systems may have varying formats, structures, and standards, making it challenging to combine and analyze effectively. To overcome this challenge, organizations must implement data governance frameworks that define data standards, ensure data integrity, and eliminate silos across systems. Data integration tools and APIs can also help bridge the gap between AI systems and existing software platforms, ensuring seamless data flow.

System Compatibility and Integration

Many organizations have legacy systems that were not designed with AI integration in mind. These systems can be difficult to modify or integrate with modern AI technologies. Overcoming system compatibility challenges may require organizations to invest in middleware or integration platforms that facilitate communication between AI solutions and legacy systems.

Additionally, some ERP, WMS, and TMS systems may not have the necessary capabilities or open interfaces to support AI integration. In such cases, organizations may need to consider upgrading their existing systems to AI-enabled versions or selecting third-party AI integration platforms that are specifically designed to work with legacy systems.

Employee Buy-in and Change Management

Integrating AI into existing supply chain systems can be disruptive, particularly for employees who are used to traditional ways of working. Employees may be resistant to change, fearing job displacement or loss of control over decision-making processes.

To overcome this challenge, organizations must focus on change management strategies. This includes educating employees about the benefits of AI, involving them in the integration process, and providing adequate training to help them adapt to new workflows and AI tools. Change management efforts should emphasize the role of AI as an augmentation tool that supports decision-making rather than replacing human workers.

System Integration Testing

Before deploying AI across the organization, it is essential to conduct thorough system integration testing to ensure that AI solutions work seamlessly with existing ERP, WMS, and TMS systems. Testing should focus on identifying potential system conflicts, data inconsistencies, and integration errors.

Successful testing requires a collaborative approach between IT teams, AI experts, and business units. Testing should be comprehensive, involving real-world scenarios that simulate supply chain processes and validate the performance of AI solutions in operational environments.

Ongoing Monitoring and Support

AI systems require continuous monitoring and maintenance to ensure that they continue to perform optimally. This is particularly important when integrating AI with legacy systems, where any changes to the underlying infrastructure or software can impact AI performance.

Organizations must establish robust monitoring frameworks to track the performance of AI models, ensuring that they deliver accurate predictions and recommendations. Additionally, technical support teams must be prepared to troubleshoot issues that arise from system integration, ensuring minimal disruption to supply chain operations.

Conclusion

Integrating AI with existing ERP, WMS, and TMS systems is essential for unlocking the full potential of AI in supply chain management. While compatibility challenges exist, these can be overcome with the right technical expertise, strategic planning, and ongoing support. By ensuring that AI is effectively integrated into existing systems, organizations can automate routine tasks, improve decision-making, and drive greater efficiencies throughout their supply chains. As AI continues to evolve, organizations that successfully navigate the integration process will gain a competitive edge, enhancing their ability to adapt to changing market conditions and customer demands.

14. Managing Data for AI Success

The success of Artificial Intelligence (AI) in any supply chain operation hinges significantly on how well data is collected, processed, cleaned, and maintained. AI models are heavily reliant on high-quality data to make accurate predictions, optimize processes, and deliver insights. Managing data effectively ensures that AI systems function optimally and deliver the anticipated benefits to an organization. This chapter explores how to manage data for AI success, focusing on data collection and cleaning processes, as well as ensuring data security and privacy.

Data Collection and Cleaning

In the context of AI, data collection is the first critical step. For AI to function effectively, it needs access to a large volume of relevant data that is continuously updated. However, the sheer volume of data involved in AI applications, along with the need for diverse and high-quality data sources, can present significant challenges. Collecting data in a structured and meaningful way is crucial for building accurate AI models.

Data collection involves gathering data from various sources, which may include operational systems such as Enterprise Resource Planning (ERP), Warehouse Management Systems (WMS), Transportation Management Systems (TMS), sensors, Internet of Things (IoT) devices, and even external data sources such as market trends and customer behavior. These data sources can provide valuable inputs for AI models, allowing organizations to better predict demand, optimize inventory, enhance supplier relationships, and improve overall supply chain management.

However, data collected from multiple systems can often be inconsistent, incomplete, or fragmented. This can undermine the quality and effectiveness of AI systems, leading to suboptimal predictions or even faulty conclusions. Therefore, data cleaning is an essential step in preparing data for AI applications.

Data cleaning refers to the process of identifying and correcting errors, inconsistencies, and inaccuracies in the data before it is used in AI models. The goal of data cleaning is to ensure that the data is accurate, reliable, and complete. Common data quality issues include:

- **Duplicate Records**: Redundant data entries can lead to skewed analysis and incorrect predictions. Identifying and removing duplicates is vital to maintaining data integrity.
- **Missing Data**: Incomplete datasets can affect AI model performance. Missing data may result from system errors or inadequate data collection processes. Depending on the nature of the missing data, it may be imputed using statistical methods, or in some cases, entire records may need to be removed.
- **Inconsistent Data Formats**: Data collected from multiple sources often comes in different formats. This inconsistency must be addressed by standardizing data formats to ensure compatibility across datasets.
- **Outliers**: Extreme values in the data that do not reflect the usual patterns can lead to inaccurate predictions or skewed analyses. Outliers must be identified and dealt with appropriately, either through correction, removal, or careful handling in the AI model.
- **Data Validation**: Ensuring that the data being collected is valid for the task at hand is crucial. Invalid or irrelevant data should be removed, as it can negatively impact model training and predictive accuracy.

Data cleaning is an ongoing process, especially in dynamic supply chains where conditions change frequently. Organizations must implement processes to clean data in real time or on a regular schedule, ensuring that data remains accurate and up-to-date for AI models.

Once data cleaning is complete, organizations can proceed to the next step: preparing the data for AI models. This involves organizing the cleaned data into a format suitable for analysis, which may include feature engineering, normalizing data, and transforming data into the right structure for machine learning algorithms. Data preparation sets the foundation for AI models to learn from historical data and generate accurate predictions or insights.

Ensuring Data Security and Privacy

Data security and privacy are paramount considerations when managing data for AI applications. With the rise of AI and the increasing reliance on data-driven decision-making, organizations must ensure that the data they collect and process is protected from breaches, theft, or misuse. Additionally, in many regions, there are legal and regulatory requirements regarding data privacy that organizations must adhere to. Failure to comply with these regulations can result in significant legal and financial repercussions.

Data Security

AI models depend on large datasets, which may include sensitive information such as customer data, supplier details, transaction histories, and proprietary business information. Securing this data is crucial to prevent unauthorized access or breaches that could lead to reputational damage, financial loss, or legal consequences.

One of the key principles of data security is **access control**. Organizations must define clear access control policies that limit who can access data based on roles and responsibilities. For instance, only authorized personnel should have access to sensitive customer or financial data. Implementing role-based access controls (RBAC) ensures that only individuals who need the data to perform their job functions can access it. Moreover, **multi-factor authentication (MFA)** and **encryption** can be used to further safeguard data access.

Another important aspect of data security is **data encryption**. Encryption protects data both in transit (as it moves across networks) and at rest (when it is stored in databases). By encrypting sensitive data, organizations reduce the risk of unauthorized access, ensuring that even if data is intercepted or accessed by malicious actors, it remains unreadable without the decryption key.

Regular **security audits** and vulnerability assessments are also crucial for ensuring data security. Organizations should conduct periodic security reviews to identify and mitigate potential risks, ensuring that data security measures remain robust and up to date. Additionally, **data masking** techniques can be used to anonymize sensitive data, especially when using datasets for AI model training. This reduces the risk of exposing personal or confidential information while still allowing for the effective use of data.

Data Privacy

Alongside data security, organizations must also focus on ensuring **data privacy**. Privacy concerns are particularly important when dealing with personal data, such as customer information or employee records. Several laws and regulations exist around the world to govern the collection, processing, and storage of personal data, including the **General Data Protection Regulation (GDPR)** in the European Union and the **California Consumer Privacy Act (CCPA)** in the United States. These regulations mandate that organizations handle personal data responsibly, giving individuals control over how their data is used.

One of the fundamental principles of data privacy is **data minimization**. This means that organizations should only collect and process the data necessary for the task at hand. For example, AI models designed for demand forecasting may only need access to sales data, inventory levels, and supplier performance data, but not personal customer details. By minimizing data collection, organizations reduce the risk of violating privacy laws or exposing sensitive information.

Another important principle is **transparency**. Organizations must inform individuals about how their data will be collected, used, and stored. Consent should be obtained from data subjects before their personal data is used in AI models, and they should be given the opportunity to withdraw consent at any time. Clear privacy policies and user agreements are essential for ensuring transparency and fostering trust with customers, employees, and other stakeholders.

Data Anonymization and De-Identification

In many cases, data anonymization or de-identification techniques can be used to protect privacy while still enabling AI models to generate valuable insights. These techniques involve removing or obfuscating personally identifiable information (PII) from datasets, ensuring that individuals cannot be identified from the data. Anonymized data can be used for AI model training without violating privacy regulations, allowing organizations to make data-driven decisions while protecting customer and employee information.

However, it's important to note that even anonymized data must be handled carefully. Organizations should regularly assess whether anonymization techniques are sufficient to protect privacy, especially as AI models become more sophisticated and the risk of re-identification increases.

Ensuring that anonymization processes are effective is critical to safeguarding personal data.

Compliance with Regulatory Requirements

As organizations collect and use data for AI purposes, they must be aware of the regulatory environment surrounding data privacy and security. In addition to GDPR and CCPA, there may be other local, national, or industry-specific regulations that govern data usage. Non-compliance with these regulations can result in significant fines and damage to the organization's reputation.

Organizations must maintain thorough records of data collection, processing, and usage activities to demonstrate compliance with privacy regulations. Regular training and awareness programs for employees are also crucial to ensure that everyone in the organization understands their responsibilities regarding data privacy and security.

Conclusion

Managing data effectively is essential for the success of AI in supply chain operations. Data collection, cleaning, and preparation form the foundation for building reliable AI models, while robust data security and privacy practices ensure that the data is protected and compliant with regulations. By implementing strong data management practices, organizations can maximize the value of their AI initiatives, improving efficiency, optimizing supply chain processes, and enhancing decision-making. As the reliance on AI continues to grow, managing data with the utmost care and responsibility will remain a key determinant of success.

15. Scaling AI Solutions Across the Supply Chain

As organizations increasingly turn to Artificial Intelligence (AI) to drive improvements in their supply chains, scaling AI solutions from pilot projects to full implementation becomes a crucial step in realizing their long-term benefits. The successful deployment of AI technology across an entire supply chain requires careful planning, consistent execution, and a focus on maintaining alignment across regions and functions. This chapter will explore how organizations can effectively scale AI solutions, transitioning from pilot initiatives to full-scale adoption, and ensuring consistency in execution across different regions and departments.

Moving from Pilot Projects to Full Implementation

Many organizations begin their AI journey with pilot projects that focus on solving specific challenges or optimizing certain supply chain functions. These pilot projects allow companies to experiment with AI technologies on a smaller scale, test their potential, and assess the effectiveness of AI models in real-world scenarios. However, moving from a pilot to full-scale implementation requires careful consideration of several factors to ensure success.

The first step in scaling AI is to **validate the success of the pilot**. This validation phase involves evaluating the performance of the AI solution against predefined success metrics, such as cost savings, improved efficiency, enhanced decision-making, or improved customer satisfaction. If the pilot project meets or exceeds expectations, the organization can proceed with expanding the use of AI across the supply chain. If the results are mixed or underwhelming, companies may need to adjust their approach, refine their models, or reconsider which AI technologies are most applicable.

Once the pilot project has been successfully validated, the next step is to **develop a clear roadmap for scaling AI**. This roadmap should outline the key milestones, timelines, resources, and budget required to expand AI use across the organization. The roadmap should also define the expected outcomes for each phase of the rollout, such as improved demand forecasting, optimized inventory management, or more efficient transportation routes.

A critical component of scaling AI is ensuring that the technology is not only effective in the initial pilot location or function but is also **adaptable to the broader supply chain environment**. This involves assessing the various supply chain functions that could benefit from AI, including procurement, logistics, warehousing, inventory management, and supplier relationship management, and prioritizing them for expansion. Each function has its own unique set of challenges, data requirements, and performance metrics, which means that AI models must be customized or reconfigured to address the specific needs of each area.

Organizations should also **ensure that the necessary infrastructure** is in place to support the scaling of AI solutions. This includes investing in cloud-based platforms, data storage solutions, and computing power that can handle the increased data volume and processing demands as AI models are deployed across multiple functions. AI also requires robust data pipelines, which may need to be enhanced to ensure that accurate and up-to-date data is available for machine learning models at scale.

Training is another critical factor in successfully scaling AI. As AI is integrated into more parts of the organization, employees will need to be trained on how to interact with the technology, understand its outputs, and make data-driven decisions based on AI recommendations. This includes not only supply chain professionals but also IT teams who will manage the infrastructure and data, and decision-makers who must trust AI-generated insights to guide strategic actions.

Ensuring Consistency Across Regions/Functions

One of the biggest challenges organizations face when scaling AI across a global supply chain is ensuring **consistency across regions and functions**. A supply chain that spans multiple countries and regions often involves different cultural contexts, operational processes, regulatory requirements, and technological infrastructures. To achieve consistent performance across all regions, it is essential to standardize processes and align goals, all while maintaining flexibility to adapt to local conditions.

The first step in ensuring consistency is to **align AI solutions with overall business objectives**. Scaling AI should not be done in isolation but as part of a broader strategy that ties AI adoption to the company's supply chain goals. These goals should be consistent across all regions and functions to ensure that AI solutions address the same challenges and deliver similar outcomes, such as improved efficiency, cost reduction, or enhanced customer service.

To maintain consistency, organizations must implement **standardized processes and workflows** across regions. This includes defining common standards for data collection, reporting, and performance measurement. By establishing uniformity in these key areas, organizations can ensure that AI models are trained using the same data standards and that the results generated by AI systems are comparable across functions and regions.

In addition to standardizing data and processes, organizations must also ensure **consistent integration of AI with existing systems and tools** across regions. Whether using Enterprise Resource Planning (ERP) systems, Warehouse

Management Systems (WMS), or Transportation Management Systems (TMS), it is important to ensure that AI tools can seamlessly integrate with these existing technologies to deliver consistent outputs. A uniform integration strategy across regions ensures that all parts of the supply chain are working with the same AI-enabled tools and technologies, regardless of location.

Building a Global Data Strategy

A successful AI rollout across multiple regions requires a **global data strategy** that accounts for the nuances of local operations. While data may be collected and processed locally, it should be centralized and standardized where possible to ensure consistency. This can be achieved by using a **centralized data warehouse** or **cloud-based data management platform** that integrates data from all regions and makes it accessible to AI models. Centralization allows for more accurate, comprehensive, and actionable insights that can be leveraged across the entire supply chain.

Organizations must also consider **regional data privacy and regulatory requirements** when scaling AI. Different regions may have different rules regarding data protection, such as the **General Data Protection Regulation (GDPR)** in Europe or **California Consumer Privacy Act (CCPA)** in the United States. AI models that rely on personal data may need to be adjusted or reconfigured to comply with these regulations, ensuring that data is handled securely and ethically across all regions.

Maintaining Organizational Alignment

As AI is scaled across the supply chain, it's essential to **maintain organizational alignment** across all functions. This means engaging stakeholders from all departments involved in the supply chain, including procurement, logistics, warehousing, IT, and finance, to ensure that everyone understands the value and role of AI in the organization's overall strategy. Regular communication, training, and feedback loops help keep all departments aligned with the business objectives and AI's role in achieving them.

One effective way to maintain alignment is through the formation of an **AI center of excellence (CoE)** within the organization. The CoE serves as a central hub for driving AI adoption, providing best practices, and facilitating knowledge sharing across regions and functions. The CoE ensures that all teams have access to the tools, resources, and expertise necessary to effectively use AI and scale its impact.

In addition to organizational alignment, it is important to foster a **culture of collaboration**. AI adoption often requires cross-functional collaboration, as AI models typically span multiple supply chain functions. Encouraging a culture where teams work together and share insights ensures that AI is deployed efficiently and effectively across the organization.

Continuous Improvement and Monitoring

Even after scaling AI across the supply chain, organizations must **continuously monitor and improve** their AI models to maintain their effectiveness. This includes regularly evaluating the performance of AI systems, monitoring their impact on key metrics, and collecting feedback from users. AI models should be retrained and refined as new data becomes available, ensuring that they continue to provide accurate insights as market conditions, consumer behavior, and supply chain dynamics evolve.

In addition, organizations must establish **feedback loops** that allow employees at all levels to provide input on the AI solutions. This helps ensure that AI systems are delivering the desired results and are adjusted if needed. Engaging employees in this way also helps foster trust in AI and demonstrates that it is a tool for enhancing, rather than replacing, human expertise.

Conclusion

Scaling AI solutions across the supply chain is a challenging but necessary step in fully realizing the potential of AI technologies. The key to success lies in moving from pilot projects to full implementation through careful planning, infrastructure investments, and employee training. To ensure consistency across regions and functions, organizations must standardize processes, integrate AI seamlessly with existing systems, and maintain alignment with business objectives. With a strong focus on data management, regulatory compliance, and continuous improvement, organizations can scale AI solutions effectively, driving efficiency, innovation, and a competitive edge across their global supply chains.

Part 4: Challenges and Solutions

16. Common Barriers to AI Adoption

The adoption of Artificial Intelligence (AI) within the supply chain is a transformative process that brings immense potential benefits, such as improved efficiency, cost reduction, and enhanced decision-making capabilities. However, like any major technological shift, AI adoption is not without its challenges. Organizations frequently encounter several barriers that can impede the smooth integration and scaling of AI solutions across their supply chains. Two of the most common barriers are **resistance to change** and **budget and resource constraints**. This chapter explores these challenges in detail and provides insights into how organizations can overcome them.

Resistance to Change

One of the most pervasive barriers to AI adoption is **resistance to change** within the organization. Employees, managers, and even leadership can be hesitant to embrace AI technologies due to a variety of reasons, including fear of job displacement, concerns about the complexity of AI systems, and a general resistance to altering established workflows.

1. **Fear of Job Displacement**: One of the primary reasons for resistance to AI adoption is the fear that automation and AI solutions will replace human jobs. Many employees fear that AI-driven systems, which can perform tasks like data analysis, predictive modeling, and inventory management, will render their roles redundant. This fear can lead to reluctance in accepting AI systems, resulting in passive resistance or active opposition to the change.

   Solution: To address this concern, organizations must emphasize that AI is intended to augment human capabilities, not replace them. AI technologies can automate repetitive tasks and handle large volumes of data, freeing up employees to focus on more strategic, value-added activities. Organizations should communicate clearly that AI adoption will enhance their jobs by providing better tools, increasing efficiency, and enabling more data-driven decision-making. Additionally, organizations should focus on **upskilling** and **reskilling** employees to work alongside AI, ensuring that they are equipped with the knowledge and skills needed to leverage new technologies.

2. **Lack of Trust in AI**: Some employees may resist AI because they do not trust the technology or the predictions it generates. AI systems rely on algorithms and data patterns that can be difficult for non-technical stakeholders to understand, leading to skepticism about their accuracy and reliability.

   Solution: Building trust in AI requires transparency and communication. Organizations should make an effort to **educate** employees on how AI works, the benefits it brings, and how decisions are made. This can be achieved through training sessions, workshops, and hands-on demonstrations that show AI's real-world applications in supply chain management. Engaging employees in the AI implementation process and showing them tangible results from pilot projects can also foster trust in the technology.

3. **Cultural Resistance**: Resistance to change is often deeply ingrained in organizational culture. Employees may be accustomed to traditional methods of doing things, and the introduction of AI can feel disruptive to the established way of working. Additionally, leaders may be hesitant to push for AI adoption if they fear that their teams will resist or that the technology may not deliver immediate results.

Solution: Overcoming cultural resistance requires a **change management strategy** that involves leadership, communication, and a clear vision. Leaders should champion the adoption of AI, acting as role models and encouraging their teams to embrace the change. Moreover, organizations should implement AI gradually, allowing employees to become familiar with the technology at their own pace. Incremental AI adoption and setting small, achievable goals can help ease the transition and reduce the fear of the unknown.

Budget and Resource Constraints

The second major barrier to AI adoption in supply chain management is **budget and resource constraints**. Implementing AI solutions requires significant financial investment, as well as the allocation of resources in terms of skilled personnel, infrastructure, and ongoing maintenance. These costs can be a major hurdle, particularly for small and mid-sized companies that may not have the financial flexibility to invest in such advanced technologies.

1. **High Initial Investment Costs**: AI technologies, especially when tailored to the unique needs of a supply chain, can come with a hefty price tag. This includes the costs of purchasing AI software, acquiring the necessary hardware, and engaging with external vendors or consultants for AI system development. For many organizations, these upfront costs can seem prohibitive, leading to delays in AI adoption or a reluctance to invest in AI altogether.

    Solution: To address the high initial costs, organizations should view AI as a long-term investment rather than an immediate expenditure. The ROI of AI solutions in supply chain management can be significant, with improvements in efficiency, inventory management, demand forecasting, and customer service. To minimize costs, companies can consider **cloud-based AI solutions** and **Software-as-a-Service (SaaS)** models, which allow businesses to access AI technologies without the need for large capital investments in hardware and infrastructure. Additionally, organizations can explore **pilot projects** and **phased rollouts**, which help spread costs over time and allow for more gradual implementation.

2. **Lack of Skilled Talent**: AI systems require skilled personnel to develop, implement, and maintain them. These professionals, including data scientists, machine learning engineers, and AI specialists, are in high demand, and the shortage of skilled talent can create budgetary and resource challenges. Organizations may struggle to find or afford the right expertise, leading to delays or suboptimal AI implementations.

   Solution: Companies can overcome the talent shortage by **training existing employees** in AI-related skills. By investing in **upskilling** and **reskilling** programs, organizations can prepare their current workforce to take on new roles related to AI. This approach helps reduce recruitment costs while building internal capabilities. Additionally, organizations can explore **partnerships** with universities, research institutions, or external AI experts to access the necessary skills without having to hire full-time employees. **Outsourcing** certain aspects of AI development to third-party vendors is another option for companies with limited internal resources.

3. **Integration with Existing Systems**: Integrating AI with existing supply chain systems, such as Enterprise Resource Planning (ERP) software, Warehouse

Management Systems (WMS), and Transportation Management Systems (TMS), can be resource-intensive. AI models often require data from multiple sources, and aligning AI systems with existing infrastructure can necessitate significant investment in IT support and system upgrades.

Solution: To manage integration costs, organizations should focus on choosing AI solutions that are compatible with their existing systems. Many AI vendors offer solutions that integrate seamlessly with common supply chain technologies, reducing the need for extensive IT redevelopment. Additionally, companies can explore **modular AI solutions** that can be implemented in stages, starting with the areas that are most critical or have the highest potential for improvement. This phased approach reduces the upfront investment and allows for a smoother integration process.

4. **Ongoing Maintenance and Support Costs**: AI systems require continuous monitoring, maintenance, and updates to ensure they remain accurate and effective. The need for ongoing resources for system updates, data management, and AI model retraining can add to the overall cost of AI adoption.

Solution: To mitigate ongoing costs, organizations should **plan for long-term support and maintenance** when budgeting for AI implementation. This includes allocating resources for data storage, processing, and model maintenance. Additionally, companies can consider **AI solutions with built-in support**, which offer ongoing updates and troubleshooting as part of the service. Developing a strong internal team or partnering with AI vendors for long-term maintenance contracts can help control costs and ensure the continued success of the AI system.

Conclusion

AI adoption in supply chain management presents significant opportunities for organizations to enhance operational efficiency, reduce costs, and improve decision-making. However, the barriers to AI adoption—such as resistance to change and budget/resource constraints—must be addressed in order to fully realize the potential of AI technologies. Overcoming resistance requires effective change management strategies, clear communication, and upskilling programs to build trust and encourage acceptance of AI. Similarly, addressing budget and resource challenges involves considering alternative financial models, training internal talent, and ensuring that AI solutions can integrate with existing systems. By proactively addressing these barriers, organizations can accelerate AI adoption and unlock the transformative benefits that AI offers to the supply chain.

17. Overcoming Ethical and Compliance Concerns

As Artificial Intelligence (AI) continues to revolutionize supply chain management, it introduces a range of ethical and compliance concerns that must be addressed to ensure responsible, transparent, and fair use of the technology. While AI can significantly enhance efficiency, accuracy, and decision-making, its adoption also raises important questions related to fairness, accountability, transparency, privacy, and legal compliance. In this chapter, we will explore two primary challenges organizations must overcome to ensure AI is used ethically and in compliance with regulations: **addressing bias in AI systems** and **ensuring regulatory compliance in AI use**.

Addressing Bias in AI Systems

Bias in AI systems is one of the most significant ethical concerns facing organizations today. AI algorithms are designed to analyze vast amounts of data and make decisions or predictions based on that data. However, if the data fed into AI systems contains biases—whether due to historical inequalities, imbalanced datasets, or human prejudices—the AI may perpetuate or even amplify these biases in its decision-making processes. This can result in unfair outcomes, discriminatory practices, and reputational damage for organizations, especially in sensitive areas like hiring, procurement, supplier selection, and demand forecasting.

1. **Types of Bias in AI Systems**:
   There are several types of bias that can creep into AI systems. These include:
   - **Data Bias**: AI models are only as good as the data they are trained on. If the data used to train an AI system is biased, the system will learn and replicate those biases. For example, if an AI model used for supplier selection is trained on data that reflects historical patterns of favoring certain geographic regions or supplier

demographics, the system may inadvertently perpetuate those biases.
- **Algorithmic Bias**: Bias can also arise from the algorithms themselves. Even if the data is unbiased, the way the algorithm processes that data can introduce biases. This is often due to flaws in the model's design, unintended correlations, or assumptions made during model development.
- **Feedback Loop Bias**: AI systems can create feedback loops where biased outcomes feed back into the system and reinforce the original bias. For example, if an AI-based demand forecasting system overestimates the demand for a particular product due to biased historical data, it could lead to inflated production or stocking levels, which in turn reinforces the demand patterns in the AI model.

2. **Mitigating Bias in AI**:
To mitigate bias, organizations need to focus on several key strategies:
- **Diverse and Representative Data**: One of the most effective ways to prevent bias is to ensure that the data used to train AI models is **diverse, representative**, and free from discriminatory patterns. Organizations should use data that reflects the real-world diversity of their supply chain, customers, and suppliers, ensuring that all groups are fairly represented. This includes considering demographic factors such as gender, race, geography, and socio-economic status when developing datasets.
- **Bias Audits and Testing**: Regular audits and testing of AI models are crucial for identifying and addressing bias. Organizations should implement **bias detection frameworks** and tools that can help identify biased patterns in the

data and the outputs of AI systems. By performing audits at different stages of AI development—such as during training, validation, and deployment—organizations can detect and correct any biases before they impact business operations.
- **Bias Mitigation Algorithms**: There are various **bias mitigation techniques** that can be implemented during the model development process. These include adjusting the training data to reduce bias, modifying the model's learning algorithm to account for fairness, and using post-processing methods to ensure that biased decisions are not made during deployment. Organizations should partner with data scientists and AI developers who specialize in **fairness-aware machine learning** techniques to ensure that their models are as unbiased as possible.
- **Transparency and Explainability**: Ensuring transparency and explainability in AI systems can help uncover potential biases. By providing explanations for AI-generated decisions, organizations can better understand the reasoning behind them and assess whether bias is influencing the outcomes. This approach also helps build trust among stakeholders, as they can see that AI systems are making decisions based on objective and fair criteria.

3. **Ethical Implications of AI Bias**:
The ethical implications of biased AI systems are far-reaching. Bias in AI can perpetuate existing societal inequalities and create unfair outcomes for certain groups. In the context of supply chain management, AI-driven decisions that are biased against specific suppliers, regions, or products can lead to missed opportunities, exclusion, and unequal treatment. This

not only damages a company's reputation but can also have legal and financial consequences, particularly in industries with strict anti-discrimination regulations.

Organizations must acknowledge their responsibility in ensuring that AI systems are designed and deployed in a manner that aligns with ethical principles of fairness, justice, and non-discrimination. This means actively working to eliminate bias, promoting diversity in the supply chain, and ensuring that AI is used to support **inclusive decision-making**.

Regulatory Compliance in AI Use

As AI technologies continue to evolve, regulatory bodies are increasingly focusing on ensuring that AI systems are used in ways that protect privacy, ensure fairness, and promote transparency. Organizations must navigate a complex landscape of local, national, and international regulations that govern the use of AI, particularly in the context of sensitive supply chain operations such as procurement, sourcing, and logistics.

1. **Global AI Regulations**:
    The regulatory environment for AI is still developing, but several major frameworks and guidelines have been established at the global level. Some of the most prominent regulations include:
    - **General Data Protection Regulation (GDPR)**: The European Union's GDPR is one of the most well-known regulations that impacts AI, particularly in terms of data privacy and protection. The GDPR places strict requirements on organizations that collect and process personal data, including data used to train AI systems. AI systems that process personal data must comply with principles such as **data**

minimization, **transparency**, and **consent**, and they must provide individuals with rights to access, rectify, and erase their data.
- **AI Act (EU)**: The European Commission's proposed AI Act is another important regulatory framework aimed at ensuring the safe and ethical use of AI. This regulation classifies AI systems into four risk categories (from minimal to high risk) and sets out different obligations depending on the level of risk posed by the AI system. Organizations must comply with requirements related to transparency, human oversight, and accountability for high-risk AI applications.
- **Algorithmic Transparency Laws**: Various countries are introducing laws that require organizations to provide transparency about how their AI systems work and the decisions they make. For example, some jurisdictions are considering regulations that require companies to disclose the use of automated decision-making systems, as well as provide explanations for AI-generated decisions that affect individuals or businesses.

2. **Ensuring Compliance with Regulatory Frameworks**:
   To ensure compliance with these regulations, organizations must adopt several key strategies:
   - **Data Privacy Management**: Organizations must ensure that their AI systems comply with data protection regulations such as the GDPR. This involves implementing strong data governance practices, ensuring that data is collected and used lawfully, and securing explicit consent from individuals where necessary. Data used to train AI models must be anonymized or pseudonymized to protect privacy, and

organizations must have robust systems in place to handle data access requests from individuals.
- **AI System Audits**: Regular audits of AI systems are essential for ensuring compliance with regulatory requirements. These audits should assess the AI system's alignment with data privacy laws, fairness standards, and transparency obligations. Independent third-party audits can provide an added layer of accountability, helping organizations ensure that they are meeting legal and ethical standards.
- **Ethical AI Frameworks**: Organizations should adopt ethical AI frameworks that align with regulatory requirements while also upholding their own ethical standards. These frameworks should incorporate principles such as fairness, accountability, transparency, and non-discrimination. By embedding ethical considerations into the AI development process, organizations can ensure that their AI systems comply with both legal and moral guidelines.
- **Training and Awareness**: It is crucial to train employees at all levels of the organization on the importance of regulatory compliance and ethical AI practices. This includes educating staff on relevant laws and guidelines, as well as creating a culture of responsibility and accountability when it comes to AI decision-making.

3. **Legal Liability and Risk Management**:
Failure to comply with AI regulations can expose organizations to legal liability and reputational risks. This includes potential fines, legal actions from affected individuals or organizations, and loss of consumer trust. By proactively managing legal compliance and ethical considerations, organizations can minimize these risks and create a more sustainable and responsible AI ecosystem.

Conclusion

As AI continues to be integrated into supply chain management, organizations must address the ethical and compliance challenges associated with its adoption. Bias in AI systems must be mitigated through diverse and representative data, algorithmic fairness, and transparency. Additionally, organizations must navigate complex regulatory frameworks to ensure compliance with data protection laws, AI regulations, and ethical standards. By addressing these challenges head-on, organizations can ensure that AI is used in a responsible, transparent, and compliant manner, ultimately fostering trust, fairness, and accountability across their supply chain operations.

18. Dealing with Technological Challenges

As organizations increasingly adopt Artificial Intelligence (AI) to optimize supply chain management, they face numerous technological challenges that must be addressed for the successful implementation and long-term viability of AI solutions. The integration of AI technologies into supply chain processes is not a simple plug-and-play operation; it requires careful management to ensure that systems remain operational, secure, and up to date. Two of the primary technological challenges organizations face are **handling system failures and maintenance** and **keeping up with rapidly evolving AI technologies**. In this chapter, we will explore these challenges in detail and offer strategies to mitigate risks and ensure the smooth operation of AI systems.

Handling System Failures and Maintenance

AI systems, while powerful and efficient, are complex and susceptible to failure. When AI-powered supply chain solutions fail, the consequences can be severe, ranging from disrupted operations and increased costs to damaged relationships with customers and suppliers. To minimize the risk of system failures and ensure consistent performance, organizations must be prepared with robust strategies for maintenance, troubleshooting, and recovery.

1. **Understanding the Causes of System Failures**
   There are several potential causes of AI system failures, including:
   - **Hardware Failures**: AI systems rely heavily on computing infrastructure, such as servers, storage systems, and networking equipment. A failure in any of these components can result in system downtime or degraded performance, disrupting supply chain operations.

- **Software Bugs and Errors**: AI algorithms, while designed to optimize processes, are also prone to errors in the code or algorithmic logic. Bugs in the software can lead to incorrect predictions, inefficient processes, or even system crashes. These issues may arise during the initial deployment or as a result of updates and changes to the system.
- **Data Inconsistencies or Corruption**: AI systems rely on high-quality data to make accurate predictions and decisions. If the input data is incomplete, inconsistent, or corrupted, the AI system may malfunction, leading to errors in forecasting, inventory management, or supplier selection.
- **Integration Failures**: Integrating AI into existing systems, such as Enterprise Resource Planning (ERP), Warehouse Management Systems (WMS), and Transportation Management Systems (TMS), can sometimes result in compatibility issues. These integration challenges may cause disruptions in system communication, data flow, and overall operational efficiency.

2. **Strategies for Preventing System Failures**

To minimize the risk of AI system failures, organizations should implement several proactive strategies:

- **Regular System Monitoring**: One of the most effective ways to prevent failures is through continuous monitoring of AI systems. Implementing **real-time monitoring tools** can help detect potential issues, such as slowdowns, performance bottlenecks, or abnormal behavior in the system. Proactive monitoring allows organizations to identify and

address problems before they escalate into critical failures.
- **Predictive Maintenance**: Predictive maintenance techniques leverage AI and machine learning to forecast potential equipment failures before they occur. By analyzing historical data and identifying patterns that precede failures, predictive maintenance allows organizations to schedule maintenance activities at optimal times, reducing the likelihood of unexpected downtime.
- **Automated Alerts and Escalation Protocols**: AI systems should be equipped with automated alerts that notify relevant personnel when a failure or anomaly is detected. These alerts should trigger predefined escalation protocols to ensure that issues are addressed swiftly, minimizing operational disruptions. Alerts can also be set up for routine maintenance tasks, ensuring that the system remains in optimal condition.
- **Regular Software Updates and Patches**: To ensure the AI system is running smoothly, organizations should implement a regular schedule of **software updates and patches**. Keeping the software up to date ensures that any identified bugs, security vulnerabilities, or performance issues are addressed. It is also essential to test updates and patches in a controlled environment before deploying them to the live system.
- **Data Quality Assurance**: AI systems depend on accurate and reliable data. Organizations should implement robust **data governance** and **data quality assurance processes** to ensure that data used by AI models is clean, consistent, and free from errors. Regular data audits and

validation checks can help prevent issues related to corrupted or incomplete data, which can lead to system failures.
3. **Mitigating System Failures Through Disaster Recovery Plans**
Despite the best efforts to prevent failures, some disruptions are inevitable. Therefore, organizations must have comprehensive **disaster recovery plans (DRPs)** in place. A DRP outlines the steps to take in the event of a system failure or outage, including:
   - **Backup Systems and Redundancy**: Organizations should have backup systems in place, such as secondary servers, cloud storage, and failover mechanisms, to ensure continuity of operations. Redundant systems can take over in the event of a primary system failure, minimizing downtime and preventing major disruptions.
   - **Clear Communication Channels**: Effective communication is essential during a system failure. Organizations should have predefined communication protocols to notify stakeholders, including employees, suppliers, and customers, about the issue and estimated resolution time. Transparent communication helps maintain trust during unexpected disruptions.
   - **Post-Failure Analysis and Continuous Improvement**: After a system failure is resolved, organizations should conduct a thorough post-mortem analysis to identify the root causes of the issue and implement measures to prevent it from happening again. Continuous improvement processes should be integrated into the AI lifecycle to ensure that failures lead to valuable learning opportunities.

Keeping Up with Rapidly Evolving AI Technologies

AI technology is evolving at an unprecedented rate, with new developments and innovations emerging regularly. As AI continues to advance, organizations face the challenge of keeping up with these changes to ensure they are leveraging the most cutting-edge tools and techniques. Staying ahead of the curve is crucial for maintaining competitive advantage, improving operational efficiency, and meeting the evolving needs of the supply chain.

1. **Understanding the Pace of AI Evolution**
   AI technology is not static—it evolves quickly, with advancements in areas such as machine learning algorithms, natural language processing (NLP), computer vision, and robotics. New breakthroughs are constantly reshaping how AI is applied across industries, including supply chain management. This rapid pace of change can make it difficult for organizations to stay current with the latest trends, techniques, and best practices.
2. **Challenges in Adapting to New AI Technologies**
   There are several key challenges organizations face when trying to keep up with rapidly evolving AI technologies:
   - **Investment in Continuous Learning**: AI technologies require ongoing investment in training and upskilling the workforce. As new AI tools and techniques emerge, employees need to continuously update their skills to stay relevant. However, this can be resource-intensive and time-consuming, especially for organizations with limited budgets or expertise in AI.
   - **Balancing Innovation with Stability**: While it is important to adopt the latest AI innovations, organizations must also ensure that their AI systems remain stable and functional. Rapidly

adopting new technologies without fully understanding their implications can lead to operational instability and increased risks of failure.
- **Vendor Management and Technology Partnerships**: As AI technologies evolve, organizations must carefully manage relationships with technology vendors and AI solution providers. New versions of AI software or hardware may require significant updates to existing systems or even complete replacements. Organizations need to be strategic in selecting partners who can provide the tools and support necessary to stay ahead of technological advancements.

3. **Strategies for Keeping Up with AI Technological Advancements**

To remain competitive and fully leverage the potential of AI, organizations should implement several strategies for staying up to date with technological changes:
- **Continuous Research and Development**: Organizations should allocate resources to research and development (R&D) in AI. This can involve collaborating with academic institutions, attending industry conferences, and staying informed about the latest AI research. R&D efforts help organizations anticipate emerging trends and integrate cutting-edge AI technologies into their supply chain operations.
- **Agile Adoption of New Technologies**: Instead of waiting for technologies to become fully mainstream, organizations should adopt an **agile approach** to AI technology adoption. This involves piloting new AI tools and techniques in controlled environments before rolling them out on a larger scale. By testing new technologies in

real-world scenarios, organizations can identify potential challenges and refine their strategies.
- **Building Strong Vendor Relationships**: Maintaining close relationships with AI technology vendors is essential for staying informed about product updates, new releases, and upcoming innovations. Vendors often provide training, technical support, and access to beta versions of new AI technologies, enabling organizations to stay ahead of the competition.
- **Fostering a Culture of Innovation**: Encouraging a culture of innovation within the organization can help employees stay engaged with new AI technologies. This includes creating opportunities for employees to experiment with emerging technologies, share ideas, and participate in innovation challenges. A culture of innovation fosters continuous learning and adaptation, allowing organizations to stay nimble in the face of rapid technological change.

4. **Strategic Technology Roadmap**
Developing a **technology roadmap** is an essential component of AI strategy. This roadmap outlines the steps and timelines for implementing new AI technologies and integrating them into the broader supply chain ecosystem. By mapping out the AI technology journey, organizations can prioritize investments, manage resources effectively, and stay aligned with their long-term business goals.

Conclusion

As organizations integrate AI into their supply chain operations, they must address two significant technological challenges: handling system failures and maintenance, and keeping up with rapidly evolving AI technologies. By implementing proactive maintenance strategies, investing in continuous learning, and staying agile in the face of new advancements, organizations can ensure that their AI systems remain reliable, secure, and effective. By staying ahead of technological changes and adapting to new innovations, businesses can maintain a competitive edge, optimize supply chain performance, and drive sustainable growth in the digital age.

Part 5: Future Trends in AI-Driven Supply Chains

19. The Role of IoT and Blockchain with AI

As supply chains continue to evolve and embrace digital transformation, the integration of **Internet of Things (IoT)**, **Blockchain**, and **Artificial Intelligence (AI)** is creating a powerful trifecta that enhances the efficiency, visibility, and security of supply chain operations. These technologies, when used together, enable supply chain stakeholders to manage and optimize complex processes in real-time, make more informed decisions, and ensure greater transparency and traceability. This chapter explores the role of IoT and Blockchain in enhancing AI-driven supply chains, focusing on **real-time visibility**, **enhanced traceability**, and **security**.

Real-Time Visibility and Transparency

Real-time visibility has become one of the most valuable features of modern supply chain management. Traditional supply chains often struggled with fragmented systems, leading to delays in communication and inaccurate data. The combination of **AI**, **IoT**, and **Blockchain** addresses these challenges by providing seamless, real-time data collection and sharing, allowing for accurate, timely decision-making.

1. **IoT for Real-Time Data Collection**

The **Internet of Things (IoT)** connects physical devices across the supply chain to the internet, enabling the collection and transmission of data from sensors and devices in real-time. These devices can include everything from GPS trackers on delivery vehicles to temperature sensors in warehouses, RFID tags on goods, and smart shelves in retail stores. With IoT, businesses can monitor assets, track goods, and gather performance data from different stages of the supply chain, ensuring that stakeholders have an up-to-date view of operations.

AI systems leverage this real-time data to improve decision-making processes. For instance, AI can analyze data from IoT sensors to detect anomalies or inefficiencies in the supply chain, such as delays in transportation, excessive stock levels, or equipment malfunctions. This allows businesses to take corrective actions quickly, reducing downtime and optimizing resource allocation.

2. Blockchain for Transparency and Trust

Blockchain technology further enhances the visibility of supply chain processes by offering a transparent and immutable ledger for tracking every transaction and event. In a traditional supply chain, data is stored in centralized systems that can be prone to manipulation, errors, or omissions. Blockchain, however, decentralizes the storage of transactional data, ensuring that once information is entered, it cannot be altered or deleted. This creates an auditable and verifiable trail for every part of the supply chain.

The integration of **blockchain with AI** ensures that AI models have access to reliable and accurate data. For example, when a product changes hands from a supplier to a manufacturer, the transaction is recorded on the blockchain. AI systems can then analyze the blockchain data to predict potential disruptions, optimize routes, or identify opportunities for cost savings, knowing that the information they're using is trustworthy.

Blockchain also enhances transparency in **supply chain provenance**, allowing consumers to track the entire lifecycle of a product, from raw material sourcing to final delivery. This transparency builds trust and ensures compliance with regulations, especially in industries with stringent standards, such as pharmaceuticals, food, and luxury goods.

3. AI for Decision-Making and Predictive Insights

AI integrates seamlessly with IoT and Blockchain to process large volumes of real-time data and provide actionable insights. For example, when AI algorithms have access to IoT-generated data on inventory levels, product demand, and transportation status, they can predict supply chain disruptions, such as stockouts or delays, and recommend the best course of action.

Through predictive analytics, AI can also offer **forecasting capabilities** that help businesses anticipate future demand, identify patterns in supplier performance, and optimize their inventory levels. This level of decision-making accuracy is powered by the continuous flow of data from IoT devices, and the reliability of Blockchain ensures that this data is trustworthy and secure.

Enhanced Traceability and Security

Traceability and security are critical components of an effective supply chain, particularly in industries with complex compliance requirements or when managing high-value goods. The combination of AI, IoT, and Blockchain provides an integrated solution that ensures end-to-end traceability of products while enhancing the security of data.

1. IoT for Traceability

IoT devices track the movement of goods through every stage of the supply chain. From warehouses to transportation vehicles to final delivery points, IoT-enabled products provide continuous updates on their location, condition, and status. This continuous monitoring ensures that businesses have a **real-time trace** of every product's journey, significantly reducing the risk of fraud, theft, or loss.

For example, in industries like food and pharmaceuticals, IoT-enabled temperature sensors can ensure that products are stored and transported under optimal conditions. If the temperature deviates from the specified range, IoT sensors can trigger an alert, allowing businesses to take immediate corrective action. This level of traceability improves the overall quality of goods, reduces waste, and ensures compliance with regulations.

2. Blockchain for Immutable Records

The integration of Blockchain technology takes traceability a step further by providing an immutable, transparent ledger of all supply chain transactions. Once a transaction is recorded on the Blockchain, it cannot be altered or deleted, creating an indelible record of each product's journey. This **immutable ledger** serves as proof of provenance, ensuring that all parties involved in the supply chain—suppliers, manufacturers, retailers, and consumers—can verify the authenticity and history of products.

For example, Blockchain can be used to prove the ethical sourcing of raw materials in the supply chain. By recording every step of the process, from mining to manufacturing to final distribution, Blockchain allows consumers to verify that products were sourced responsibly, free from child labor or environmentally harmful practices. This transparency helps companies comply with **regulatory standards** and build consumer trust.

3. AI for Security and Fraud Detection

While Blockchain ensures data integrity, AI enhances **data security** by identifying potential vulnerabilities and detecting fraudulent activity. AI systems can continuously monitor transactions recorded on the Blockchain and IoT data streams for unusual patterns or anomalies that might indicate fraud or cybersecurity threats.

For example, AI algorithms can analyze transaction data on the Blockchain to identify any unauthorized alterations or attempts to hack the system. Additionally, AI can help identify patterns of fraudulent behavior in supplier interactions or delivery routes, alerting supply chain managers to potential issues before they escalate.

In sectors like **luxury goods**, AI and Blockchain can work together to detect counterfeit products. Blockchain's ability to record the entire product journey ensures that the product's authenticity can be verified, while AI can analyze trends in sales or returns to identify fake products in the market.

4. **Security of IoT Devices and Blockchain Networks**

The increasing number of IoT devices connected across the supply chain also raises concerns about security. These devices generate vast amounts of sensitive data, which, if compromised, can lead to significant operational disruptions and data breaches. To address these concerns, companies need to implement robust **IoT security protocols** to protect their devices and networks from cyberattacks.

Likewise, the security of the Blockchain network itself is crucial. While Blockchain's decentralized nature offers inherent protection against tampering, organizations must ensure that the infrastructure supporting Blockchain networks is secure. This involves using cryptographic techniques to protect transaction data, adopting strong authentication methods for participants, and ensuring that smart contracts are tested and verified for vulnerabilities.

Conclusion

The convergence of **AI**, **IoT**, and **Blockchain** is transforming supply chain operations by providing real-time visibility, improving traceability, and enhancing security. These technologies work synergistically to enable smarter decision-making, more efficient operations, and greater trust among stakeholders. Real-time data collection via IoT, transparent and immutable records via Blockchain, and the predictive capabilities of AI are driving a new era of supply chain optimization.

By leveraging these technologies, organizations can not only improve operational efficiency but also gain a competitive edge in the market. The integration of IoT and Blockchain with AI represents a paradigm shift in supply chain management, and those who successfully harness these capabilities will be better equipped to navigate the challenges of the future.

20. Emerging AI Technologies for Supply Chain

As artificial intelligence (AI) continues to evolve, new technologies are emerging that hold the potential to revolutionize supply chains. These innovations, including **Generative AI** and **Quantum Computing**, are beginning to reshape how businesses optimize operations, make decisions, and create new opportunities in an increasingly complex and competitive global market. In this chapter, we explore these emerging AI technologies and their potential applications within supply chains.

Generative AI Applications

Generative AI refers to a class of AI technologies that create new data or content based on existing information. Unlike traditional AI models, which focus on analyzing data or making predictions, generative AI can generate novel outputs, such as text, images, designs, or even code. This capability is powered by advanced techniques such as **Generative Adversarial Networks (GANs)** and **Transformer-based models**.

1. Demand Forecasting and Planning

One of the key applications of generative AI in supply chains is in **demand forecasting**. Traditional forecasting models rely on historical sales data and statistical techniques to predict future demand. However, these models often struggle to account for more complex, dynamic factors such as changing consumer behavior, external disruptions, or market trends. Generative AI, on the other hand, can simulate a wide range of possible future scenarios by generating new, synthetic data based on past trends, external factors, and other variables.

For example, a generative model could be used to generate thousands of possible demand scenarios under different conditions, allowing supply chain managers to plan for a broader range of outcomes. This enables more accurate and flexible forecasting, particularly in industries subject to rapid change or uncertainty, such as fashion, electronics, or consumer goods.

2. Product Design and Customization

Generative AI is also transforming **product design** in supply chains, particularly in industries like manufacturing and automotive. By leveraging AI algorithms that learn from previous designs and customer preferences, companies can generate new product prototypes that meet specific requirements or consumer desires. In the case of 3D printing and additive manufacturing, generative AI can design optimized structures that reduce material usage while maintaining strength and durability.

For example, a car manufacturer might use generative AI to create a range of design variations for car components, considering factors like weight, aerodynamics, and cost. The AI system would then generate optimal designs that meet performance criteria while minimizing waste and production costs. This reduces the time and effort needed for manual design, speeds up the product development process, and leads to more innovative, efficient designs.

3. Supply Chain Network Design

Generative AI can be applied to optimize the overall **supply chain network** design. This includes determining the optimal locations for warehouses, distribution centers, and manufacturing facilities, considering factors like transportation costs, supplier proximity, labor availability, and environmental impact.

Using generative algorithms, businesses can generate multiple potential network configurations and evaluate their effectiveness based on different cost and performance metrics.

This approach enables companies to create more resilient and adaptable supply chains that can respond more quickly to changes in demand, supply disruptions, or geopolitical events.

4. Inventory Management

In the context of inventory management, generative AI can help create **automated replenishment systems** that are better at anticipating changes in demand. By analyzing sales data, seasonal trends, and other external factors, generative AI models can generate new inventory plans that adjust for sudden shifts in demand, promotional activities, or unexpected delays in supply.

For instance, if a retailer is expecting a surge in demand due to an upcoming holiday season, generative AI can simulate different demand scenarios and recommend adjustments to inventory levels. This can ensure that companies maintain optimal stock levels, reduce stockouts, and minimize overstock situations.

5. Generative AI for Process Optimization

Generative AI can also be employed to design and optimize supply chain processes. By using historical data on production flows, supply chain bottlenecks, and operational inefficiencies, generative models can propose new process improvements. These AI-generated solutions could involve reimagining workflows, proposing new resource allocations, or designing more efficient operational strategies, all of which can reduce costs and improve overall supply chain efficiency.

Quantum Computing in Supply Chains

Quantum computing represents a breakthrough in computational power, offering the potential to solve complex problems much faster and more efficiently than classical computers. Unlike traditional computers, which use bits to represent data as either 0 or 1, quantum computers use **quantum bits (qubits)**, which can represent multiple states simultaneously due to the principles of **quantum mechanics**. This ability to perform many calculations in parallel allows quantum computers to solve problems that are currently intractable for classical systems, especially in areas like optimization, cryptography, and data analysis.

In supply chains, quantum computing is expected to play a transformative role, particularly in areas that involve **complex decision-making**, **optimization**, and **large-scale simulations**.

1. **Optimizing Supply Chain Networks**

Supply chain optimization is one of the areas where quantum computing shows great promise. Traditional optimization algorithms struggle to process the enormous number of variables and constraints involved in designing optimal supply chain networks, such as determining the best routes for delivery trucks, the most efficient locations for warehouses, and the optimal stock levels at various points in the network.

Quantum computing can solve these types of complex optimization problems much faster by exploring many possible solutions simultaneously. For example, a quantum algorithm could be used to optimize the **vehicle routing problem** (VRP) in transportation, determining the most efficient delivery routes for a fleet of trucks across multiple cities. This level of optimization can reduce costs, improve delivery speed, and minimize environmental impact by reducing fuel consumption and emissions.

2. **Inventory Optimization and Demand Forecasting**

Another area where quantum computing can significantly impact supply chains is in **inventory optimization** and **demand forecasting**. Quantum algorithms can process vast amounts of data from multiple sources—such as historical sales, weather data, and social media trends—much more efficiently than classical algorithms. This can improve the accuracy of demand forecasts and help businesses optimize their inventory management.

For instance, a quantum computing model could simulate various demand scenarios for a product in different regions and adjust inventory levels accordingly. This would help companies reduce the risk of stockouts, minimize overstocking, and ensure that they have the right amount of inventory at the right time.

3. Supply Chain Risk Management

Supply chains are inherently vulnerable to various risks, including disruptions from natural disasters, geopolitical tensions, and supply shortages. Quantum computing can help **model and simulate** these risks more effectively, allowing businesses to prepare for and mitigate potential disruptions.

By leveraging quantum algorithms, companies can create more accurate risk models that account for multiple variables and potential outcomes. For example, quantum computing could be used to simulate the impact of a supplier going offline or a transportation route being blocked, allowing companies to develop contingency plans and alternative strategies much faster.

4. Cryptography and Security

Security and data privacy are critical concerns in the digital supply chain. As supply chains become more interconnected and rely on data from various stakeholders, the need for robust security measures becomes even more pressing. Quantum computing is expected to play a key role in **cryptography**, which is vital for securing transactions, protecting sensitive data, and ensuring compliance with regulatory requirements.

While quantum computing has the potential to break existing encryption methods, it also holds the promise of creating **quantum-resistant encryption techniques**. These new encryption methods will provide a higher level of security, ensuring that sensitive supply chain data remains protected against cyberattacks and breaches.

5. **Quantum Machine Learning for Predictive Analytics**

Quantum computing has the potential to enhance **machine learning** models used in supply chain analytics. Traditional machine learning algorithms can be computationally expensive, especially when analyzing large datasets with many variables. Quantum machine learning algorithms can potentially improve the speed and accuracy of predictive models, allowing businesses to make more informed decisions based on real-time data.

For example, a quantum-enhanced machine learning model could predict potential supply chain disruptions caused by external factors such as weather patterns, political instability, or market changes. This would enable companies to take proactive measures to address these risks and minimize their impact.

Conclusion

The integration of **Generative AI** and **Quantum Computing** into supply chain operations offers a wealth of opportunities to enhance efficiency, innovation, and resilience.

Generative AI's ability to create new data and simulate various scenarios enables more accurate demand forecasting, better product design, and process optimization. Meanwhile, Quantum Computing's vast computational power allows for the solution of complex optimization problems, improved risk management, and enhanced data security.

As these technologies continue to mature, their potential to reshape the future of supply chains becomes more apparent. Companies that embrace these emerging AI technologies will be well-positioned to gain a competitive edge, optimize their operations, and create more resilient, adaptive supply chains that can thrive in an increasingly unpredictable and dynamic global market.

21. The Impact of Autonomous Systems

The rapid advancement of **autonomous systems** is reshaping industries across the globe, and the supply chain sector is no exception. These systems, including **autonomous vehicles** and **drones**, as well as **Robotic Process Automation (RPA)**, are providing new capabilities for efficiency, speed, and cost-effectiveness. These technologies promise to revolutionize how goods are moved, handled, and managed throughout the supply chain. This chapter explores the impact of these autonomous systems on supply chains, with a focus on **autonomous vehicles and drones** and **RPA**.

Autonomous Vehicles and Drones

Autonomous vehicles and **drones** represent some of the most exciting developments in the realm of supply chain logistics. By leveraging cutting-edge technologies such as **artificial intelligence (AI)**, **machine learning (ML)**, **LiDAR**, and **computer vision**, these systems are able to navigate environments, transport goods, and make decisions without human intervention. The advent of these autonomous systems is not just about improving operational efficiency; it is about enabling new possibilities in supply chain design and management.

Autonomous Vehicles in the Supply Chain

Autonomous vehicles (AVs), including trucks and delivery vehicles, are poised to transform the way goods are transported. These vehicles rely on a combination of sensors, cameras, AI, and advanced algorithms to navigate the road, detect obstacles, and make real-time decisions. The potential applications of AVs in supply chains are vast and diverse.

1. **Long-Distance Freight and Last-Mile Delivery**

One of the primary benefits of autonomous vehicles is the ability to reduce labor costs and improve the efficiency of **long-distance freight** transportation. Autonomous trucks can operate around the clock, significantly reducing delivery times and allowing for faster shipment of goods. Since these vehicles don't require rest breaks or driver shifts, they can operate continuously, optimizing fuel usage and improving delivery consistency.

In addition to freight transportation, AVs have significant potential in **last-mile delivery**, the final leg of the supply chain journey where goods are delivered to customers. **Autonomous delivery vehicles**, including **vans** and **small robots**, can be deployed to transport packages directly to consumers. These systems are often designed to navigate urban environments, avoid traffic congestion, and deliver goods to customers' doorsteps more efficiently than traditional delivery methods. Moreover, autonomous delivery vehicles can operate in **dense urban areas** where traffic and parking constraints often slow down deliveries.

2. **Cost Reduction and Efficiency Gains**

The potential for **cost reduction** is one of the most compelling reasons to adopt autonomous vehicles in supply chains. Human labor, especially in driving, constitutes a significant portion of the transportation cost. Autonomous vehicles eliminate the need for drivers, reducing labor costs while improving delivery speed. In the long term, this leads to savings in wages, benefits, training, and insurance. Autonomous trucks also help optimize fuel consumption through more efficient driving patterns, reducing fuel costs and emissions.

Additionally, autonomous vehicles enable better **route optimization**. Using AI and data analytics, these vehicles can determine the most efficient routes for deliveries, taking into account traffic patterns, road closures, weather conditions, and other variables in real time. This capability minimizes delays, maximizes efficiency, and reduces fuel consumption.

3. Safety and Risk Reduction

Autonomous vehicles have the potential to enhance safety in supply chains by reducing the likelihood of accidents caused by human error, such as distracted driving or fatigue. With the integration of advanced sensors, AVs can detect obstacles, avoid collisions, and operate safely under varying conditions, improving safety on the roads. The reduction in accidents not only minimizes risk to human life but also lowers the costs associated with accidents, such as insurance premiums, lawsuits, and vehicle repair costs.

4. Regulatory and Infrastructure Challenges

Despite the significant benefits, there are still many **regulatory and infrastructure challenges** to overcome before the widespread adoption of autonomous vehicles in supply chains. Regulations surrounding AVs vary across regions, with some areas having strict guidelines for autonomous driving, while others are more lenient. Governments will need to update and harmonize regulations to ensure the safe and efficient deployment of AVs across borders.

Moreover, the infrastructure needed to support autonomous vehicles is still developing. To function optimally, AVs require **smart roads**, **charging stations**, and other physical infrastructure components. Until these elements are fully in place, the adoption of autonomous vehicles may be limited in some regions.

Drones in the Supply Chain

Drones, or **unmanned aerial vehicles (UAVs)**, are another autonomous technology that is transforming supply chains. Drones have been used in industries such as agriculture, construction, and defense for years, but their application in supply chain logistics is rapidly expanding. By offering the ability to move goods quickly, especially over short distances, drones are revolutionizing last-mile delivery and inventory management.

1. Last-Mile Delivery

Drones are particularly well-suited for **last-mile delivery**, the most challenging and expensive part of the logistics process. Drones can bypass road congestion, navigate over difficult terrain, and deliver packages directly to customers, often faster than traditional delivery vehicles. This is especially useful in **urban areas** with heavy traffic or **remote locations** where road infrastructure is limited.

For instance, drones can deliver essential goods, such as medicines, small electronics, or documents, to customers in urban centers, rural communities, or even disaster-stricken areas. This capability is expected to become even more critical as e-commerce continues to grow, with consumers expecting faster and more efficient delivery options.

2. Inventory Management and Warehouse Operations

Drones are also proving valuable in **inventory management** within warehouses and distribution centers. By using drones equipped with cameras, sensors, and AI, warehouses can perform **automated inventory audits**, reducing the need for manual stocktaking. Drones can quickly scan barcodes, identify discrepancies, and generate real-time inventory data.

This **automation** not only saves time but also improves **accuracy** in inventory management. Drones can operate in confined spaces or hazardous environments, enhancing warehouse efficiency without the need for human intervention. The ability to continuously monitor inventory in real-time helps businesses reduce stockouts and overstocking, improving overall supply chain performance.

3. Cost-Effective and Scalable Solutions

Drones offer a **cost-effective** solution for businesses looking to reduce logistics costs. Compared to traditional delivery methods, drones are typically less expensive to operate, as they do not require drivers, fuel, or large delivery vehicles. Moreover, drones can be easily scaled to handle increased demand during peak seasons, such as holidays or product launches, without the need for significant capital investment in infrastructure.

4. Challenges and Limitations

Despite the significant advantages, the use of drones in supply chains also faces several **challenges**. Regulatory issues are one of the biggest hurdles, as many countries have strict rules governing the use of drones, particularly in urban areas. The **Federal Aviation Administration (FAA)** in the United States, for example, has set regulations around drone flight, including restrictions on where drones can fly and how high they can travel.

Additionally, **battery life** is a limitation for drones, as most UAVs can only operate for a limited time before requiring recharging. This restriction limits the distance drones can travel and may pose challenges for longer deliveries or high-demand areas.

Robotic Process Automation (RPA)

In addition to autonomous vehicles and drones, **Robotic Process Automation (RPA)** is becoming an essential tool for enhancing supply chain operations. RPA refers to the use of software robots or "bots" to automate repetitive, manual tasks that were previously performed by humans. These tasks often involve interacting with various digital systems, entering data, generating reports, or processing transactions.

1. Streamlining Operations

RPA can significantly improve efficiency by automating **back-office operations** such as invoicing, order processing, inventory tracking, and supplier communication. These tasks, while necessary, are often time-consuming and prone to human error. By leveraging RPA, businesses can automate these processes, freeing up employees to focus on more strategic tasks.

For example, RPA can be used to automate **purchase order creation**, where the system generates and sends orders to suppliers based on inventory levels or demand forecasts. This reduces the need for manual intervention and improves order accuracy, leading to better inventory control and cost savings.

2. Improving Decision-Making

In supply chains, timely and accurate decision-making is crucial. RPA enables the **automation of decision-making processes** by providing real-time data and analytics. By integrating RPA with AI and machine learning algorithms, businesses can ensure that decisions are based on up-to-date information, improving the speed and accuracy of operations.

For instance, RPA can be used to monitor inventory levels across multiple warehouses, automatically reordering stock when it reaches predefined thresholds. This ensures that supply chains remain agile and responsive to changes in demand, minimizing the risk of stockouts or excess inventory.

3. Cost and Resource Efficiency

RPA reduces operational costs by automating repetitive tasks, which typically require a significant amount of human labor. This leads to **cost savings** and allows companies to allocate resources more effectively. Moreover, since RPA can operate 24/7, businesses can maintain continuous operations without the need for shift-based workforces, improving productivity and reducing costs.

4. Challenges in Implementing RPA

While RPA offers numerous benefits, there are challenges in its implementation. One of the primary concerns is **integration with existing systems**. For RPA to work effectively, it needs to be integrated into various software systems across the supply chain. This requires careful planning and coordination to ensure that RPA tools do not disrupt ongoing operations or lead to inefficiencies.

Additionally, there is a need for continuous **monitoring and maintenance** of RPA bots to ensure they are functioning properly and not generating errors. While RPA can handle many tasks autonomously, human oversight is still necessary to address any exceptions or unforeseen issues.

Conclusion

The integration of **autonomous vehicles, drones**, and **Robotic Process Automation (RPA)** into supply chains is driving transformative change. These technologies not only enhance efficiency, speed, and accuracy but also provide companies with the opportunity to reduce costs, improve safety, and optimize operations. However, challenges related to regulatory compliance, infrastructure, and technology integration remain. As businesses continue to adopt these autonomous systems, the impact on supply chain management will only become more pronounced, leading to a future where logistics and operations are more automated, agile, and interconnected.

22. Sustainability through AI in Supply Chain

As sustainability becomes an increasingly important priority for businesses, organizations are turning to **Artificial Intelligence (AI)** to help them meet their sustainability goals. In the context of supply chains, AI is not only transforming operational efficiency but also helping companies minimize waste, optimize resource use, and enable **green supply chains**. This chapter explores how AI is driving **sustainability** in supply chains by focusing on **optimizing resources to reduce waste** and **enabling green supply chains**.

Optimizing Resources to Reduce Waste

One of the primary ways AI contributes to **sustainability** in the supply chain is through its ability to **optimize resources** and reduce waste. The concept of waste reduction is central to sustainability, and AI technologies provide tools to minimize various forms of waste across the entire supply chain, from production to distribution.

AI in Demand Forecasting

Effective **demand forecasting** is critical in reducing waste within supply chains. Traditional forecasting methods often result in overproduction or underproduction, both of which can lead to significant waste, whether in the form of unsold goods or unmet customer demand. **AI-driven demand forecasting** uses large datasets, historical trends, and real-time information to make highly accurate predictions about customer demand. By improving the accuracy of demand forecasts, AI helps businesses plan production more effectively, minimizing overstocking and reducing waste.

For instance, AI models can consider variables like seasonal fluctuations, promotions, and macroeconomic factors that influence customer purchasing behavior. With a more accurate forecast, companies can produce the right quantity of goods, preventing excess inventory that might eventually be discarded or sold at a loss.

AI can also play a role in **dynamic demand sensing**, continuously adjusting predictions based on real-time data, such as changes in market conditions, consumer preferences, and supply disruptions. This helps businesses maintain an optimal level of inventory, reducing both waste and stockouts.

Optimizing Production Processes

AI can significantly enhance the efficiency of **manufacturing** processes by optimizing resource allocation and minimizing waste during production. AI-powered systems can monitor every step of the production process, ensuring that resources such as raw materials, energy, and labor are used efficiently.

For example, AI can help **optimize machine settings** and operational parameters, ensuring that equipment runs at peak efficiency and produces the required output with minimal waste. Through **predictive maintenance**, AI systems can detect potential equipment failures before they happen, preventing costly downtime and reducing the likelihood of defective products.

AI can also improve **material utilization** by analyzing production patterns and identifying areas where materials are being underutilized or wasted. By optimizing the way materials are cut, shaped, or assembled, AI can help reduce scrap material and minimize the environmental impact of manufacturing.

Supply Chain Optimization for Waste Reduction

AI is also transforming how supply chains themselves are **optimized** to reduce waste. Traditional supply chain networks often face challenges such as **excessive**

transportation, inefficient routing, and **underutilized storage** capacity. AI can help mitigate these challenges through **advanced optimization techniques** that ensure that goods are moved and stored in the most efficient way possible.

By using **AI-driven logistics optimization**, companies can improve the **routing of vehicles** to ensure the most fuel-efficient routes are taken, reducing carbon emissions and minimizing transportation-related waste. AI tools can also optimize **warehousing operations**, ensuring that space is used efficiently and reducing the need for excess warehouse capacity, which often leads to wasted resources.

Additionally, AI-powered **inventory management** systems can help reduce waste by maintaining the right balance of stock. These systems can identify slow-moving products and recommend actions such as bundling, discounting, or donating excess inventory, ensuring that products are used in the most efficient way possible before they reach the end of their life cycle.

Enabling Green Supply Chains

A green supply chain is one that is committed to reducing its **environmental footprint** while maintaining efficiency and profitability. AI is playing a pivotal role in enabling green supply chains by providing solutions for reducing energy consumption, minimizing carbon emissions, and promoting **circular economy** practices. By integrating AI into key areas of the supply chain, businesses can become more sustainable and environmentally friendly.

AI for Carbon Footprint Reduction

One of the most significant contributions of AI to **green supply chains** is its ability to track and reduce the **carbon**

footprint of operations. AI tools can analyze data from various sources, including transportation, production, and energy usage, to provide insights into the **carbon emissions** associated with each activity. By identifying the most carbon-intensive activities, businesses can prioritize efforts to reduce emissions and adopt more sustainable practices.

For example, AI can optimize **transportation routes**, as previously mentioned, to reduce fuel consumption and emissions. It can also help businesses choose more sustainable transportation options, such as switching from road freight to rail or sea, which are typically more energy-efficient and less polluting.

In the manufacturing process, AI can optimize **energy usage**, ensuring that factories operate at maximum efficiency and consume only the necessary amount of energy. AI can also help businesses track energy usage across their supply chains, identifying opportunities to switch to **renewable energy sources**, such as solar or wind power, further reducing the environmental impact.

Circular Economy and AI

The **circular economy** is a model that focuses on reducing waste and extending the life cycle of products by promoting **reuse, refurbishment, recycling, and upcycling**. AI is integral to the success of the circular economy by providing tools to manage materials and resources throughout their life cycle.

AI can help businesses monitor the **use and disposal** of products, ensuring that products are returned to the supply chain for **reuse or recycling**. For example, AI-powered systems can track products that are nearing the end of their life cycle, facilitating their return to manufacturers for refurbishing or remanufacturing. AI also plays a role in optimizing the **recycling process**, improving the efficiency of sorting and processing recyclable materials.

In the **reverse logistics** process, AI can help optimize the movement of used products, spare parts, or materials back through the supply chain. By automating the tracking and handling of returns, AI ensures that valuable materials are recovered and reintroduced into the production cycle rather than being disposed of.

AI can also assist in **product design** by helping companies develop products that are easier to recycle or reuse. Through **predictive modeling**, AI can analyze the life cycle of products and recommend design changes that make recycling or remanufacturing more feasible.

Supply Chain Transparency and Sustainability Reporting

Sustainability is increasingly becoming a key factor for stakeholders, including consumers, investors, and regulators. As such, businesses are under pressure to demonstrate their commitment to sustainability through **transparency** and **sustainability reporting**. AI is helping supply chain leaders meet these demands by providing tools for **real-time sustainability tracking** and reporting.

AI-driven analytics can gather data from across the supply chain, including suppliers, manufacturers, transportation providers, and customers, to provide a **comprehensive view** of the sustainability of operations. These systems can automatically collect and analyze data related to carbon emissions, water usage, waste generation, and other key sustainability metrics, allowing businesses to generate accurate, **real-time sustainability reports**.

By integrating AI with **blockchain** and **IoT**, businesses can achieve end-to-end **supply chain visibility**, enabling them to trace products and materials at every stage of the supply chain. This transparency not only ensures compliance with sustainability regulations but also allows companies to demonstrate their commitment to sustainability to consumers and other stakeholders.

Conclusion

AI is a powerful enabler of **sustainability** in supply chains, driving the optimization of resources and enabling **green practices** across industries. From reducing waste through improved demand forecasting, production optimization, and supply chain management, to helping companies reduce their carbon footprint and adopt circular economy principles, AI is transforming how businesses operate in an environmentally sustainable manner.

As the pressure for **sustainable practices** grows, AI will continue to play a critical role in helping businesses meet their environmental goals while maintaining operational efficiency. With its ability to optimize resources, reduce waste, and enable transparency, AI is shaping the future of **green supply chains**, fostering a more sustainable and responsible approach to global commerce.

23. Key Takeaways for Successful AI Implementation

As organizations increasingly turn to **Artificial Intelligence (AI)** to transform their supply chains, it is essential to understand the critical elements for successful AI adoption and implementation. AI has proven to be a powerful tool that can enhance efficiency, reduce costs, and foster innovation. However, realizing the full potential of AI in the supply chain requires careful planning, strategic alignment, and continuous improvement. Below are the key takeaways for ensuring successful AI implementation in supply chains:

1. Align AI with Business Objectives

For AI to truly add value to supply chain operations, it must be aligned with the **broader business strategy**. Whether the goal is improving efficiency, reducing costs, enhancing customer satisfaction, or driving sustainability, AI solutions should be implemented with these objectives in mind. A clear understanding of business needs will guide the selection of the right AI tools and technologies, ensuring they address the pain points most critical to the business.

Aligning AI with business goals also ensures that stakeholders across departments are invested in the AI initiative. From senior leadership to operational teams, everyone should understand how AI can impact the business, which helps foster engagement and collaboration across functions.

2. Invest in Data Quality and Management

AI is only as effective as the data it relies on. **Data quality** is paramount in ensuring the success of AI applications. Companies must focus on gathering **clean, structured, and high-quality data** that reflects accurate and up-to-date information from across the supply chain. Investing in **data**

management systems, data cleansing, and robust data governance practices is critical to avoid issues like **data silos** or inaccuracies that can undermine AI's effectiveness.

Additionally, organizations should prioritize **data integration** to enable a seamless flow of information across systems. AI relies on data from multiple sources, such as ERP systems, IoT sensors, and external suppliers. Ensuring that these data streams are connected and compatible allows AI models to generate more accurate insights and optimize operations.

3. Foster Organizational Readiness

Successful AI implementation goes beyond technology—it also requires an organizational culture that embraces change and innovation. AI adoption often encounters **resistance to change**, which can hinder progress. Companies should **train and upskill teams** to ensure they are equipped to work with AI tools and understand the new ways of working.

It is also essential to create a **culture of collaboration**, where teams from IT, data science, operations, and leadership work together to implement AI solutions. By encouraging cross-functional collaboration and continuous learning, companies can address potential challenges proactively and maximize the impact of AI.

Moreover, fostering **agility** is important when implementing AI in supply chains. AI projects should not be viewed as one-time initiatives but as ongoing, iterative processes. By adopting **agile methodologies**, businesses can experiment with AI solutions in a controlled, incremental manner, making adjustments based on real-world results and feedback.

4. Focus on Scalability

While pilot AI projects are an excellent way to test the viability of AI solutions, scaling these solutions across the supply chain is essential for achieving widespread benefits. Companies should consider **scalability** from the beginning, ensuring that AI tools are designed to handle larger datasets, more complex supply chain scenarios, and evolving business needs.

AI solutions should be **flexible and adaptable**, capable of being scaled across regions, departments, and suppliers. This requires a strong technical foundation and a clear strategy for how AI solutions will grow with the business. Additionally, **cloud-based** AI platforms can offer the scalability needed to deploy AI tools across the entire supply chain without the constraints of on-premise infrastructure.

5. Measure and Optimize AI Performance

Once AI tools are implemented, it is crucial to establish clear **performance metrics** that assess the success of the AI applications. These metrics should be aligned with the organization's strategic goals, whether that's **improving forecasting accuracy**, **optimizing inventory**, or **reducing transportation costs**.

AI performance should be continuously monitored and optimized. As AI systems gather more data and improve over time, it is important to ensure that they evolve to provide even greater value. **Regular audits** and performance reviews should be conducted to assess AI outcomes and identify opportunities for improvement.

6. Manage Ethical and Compliance Risks

As organizations implement AI, they must also consider the **ethical implications** of AI technologies. AI systems can inadvertently introduce **biases** that impact decision-making, particularly in areas such as supplier selection, risk assessment, or workforce management. Companies must ensure that AI models are **fair, transparent**, and **accountable** to mitigate potential biases.

In addition, AI systems must comply with relevant **regulations**, especially in areas like **data privacy** and **cybersecurity**. Compliance frameworks, such as GDPR or industry-specific regulations, should be integrated into the design and deployment of AI systems to ensure the responsible use of data and technology.

7. Leverage AI for Sustainability Goals

AI is not only a tool for improving supply chain efficiency but also for helping businesses achieve their **sustainability goals**. AI can assist in **reducing waste**, optimizing resource usage, and lowering carbon footprints across supply chains. Whether it's through **smart transportation routing**, **energy-efficient production processes**, or **sustainable sourcing**, AI can contribute to more sustainable practices that benefit both the business and the environment.

By integrating AI into sustainability initiatives, companies can enhance **resource optimization** and work toward a **greener supply chain**, reducing their environmental impact while meeting the increasing demand for responsible business practices from consumers, investors, and regulators.

8. Embrace Innovation and Future Technologies

AI is a rapidly evolving field, and companies must remain open to the potential of **emerging technologies**. **Generative AI**, **quantum computing**, and **autonomous systems** are just a few of the innovations that are poised to transform supply chain management further. By staying informed and continuously exploring new AI capabilities, organizations can ensure they remain competitive and adapt to the changing business landscape.

Successful AI implementation requires **strategic foresight** and the willingness to experiment with new technologies as they emerge. This mindset fosters a culture of continuous improvement and positions businesses to capitalize on the next wave of AI advancements.

9. Collaboration with Technology Partners

AI implementation in supply chains often requires specialized expertise that may not reside in-house. Partnering with **technology providers**, **consultants**, and **AI specialists** can provide access to the knowledge, tools, and resources necessary to deploy AI solutions effectively.

These partnerships can help businesses **accelerate adoption**, overcome technical challenges, and access advanced AI capabilities that may not be available internally. Working with external experts also ensures that businesses stay current with best practices and industry standards for AI adoption.

10. Cultivate Long-Term Vision and Commitment

AI is not a quick-fix solution; rather, it requires **long-term commitment** and vision. Organizations should view AI as an ongoing transformation rather than a short-term project. While the initial results may be incremental, the cumulative impact of AI over time can be **transformative**. Businesses must be patient, willing to invest in AI research and development, and committed to evolving their strategies as technology advances.

AI's true potential is realized through **continuous improvement**, with businesses constantly iterating, learning, and adapting AI systems to better meet their needs. This requires **leadership commitment**, clear governance structures, and a strong focus on aligning AI initiatives with overall business goals.

Conclusion

The journey to **successful AI implementation** in supply chains is multifaceted, involving strategic planning, investment in technology and data, organizational readiness, and ongoing optimization. By aligning AI with business objectives, fostering a culture of collaboration, ensuring data quality, and focusing on scalability, organizations can unlock the full potential of AI to transform their supply chains.

As AI continues to evolve, businesses must remain adaptable, open to innovation, and committed to the responsible and sustainable use of AI technologies. With the right approach, AI can drive significant improvements in **efficiency**, **cost-effectiveness**, **sustainability**, and **customer satisfaction**, positioning organizations for success in an increasingly competitive and data-driven marketplace.

24.The Future of AI in Supply Chain Management

The landscape of supply chain management is rapidly transforming as Artificial Intelligence (AI) continues to make a profound impact on how companies manage their supply chains. The integration of AI technologies into the supply chain offers unparalleled opportunities to enhance efficiency, reduce costs, improve customer satisfaction, and enable greater flexibility in decision-making. As we look ahead, AI's role in supply chains will continue to evolve, with new applications, challenges, and opportunities shaping the future of supply chain management.

AI's Increasing Influence in Supply Chain Evolution

AI's presence in the supply chain is expected to deepen as its capabilities expand. Traditional supply chain systems, which are often manual and siloed, are being replaced by AI-powered systems capable of automating tasks, enhancing decision-making processes, and providing real-time insights into every facet of the supply chain. **AI-driven supply chains** offer greater adaptability, resilience, and a level of intelligence that helps businesses forecast, plan, and execute operations with remarkable accuracy and speed.

The future of AI in supply chain management will likely involve the convergence of **machine learning (ML)**, **big data analytics**, and **IoT (Internet of Things)** technologies, enabling highly automated, predictive, and responsive supply chains. These technologies will continue to disrupt traditional models by delivering deeper insights, enhancing operational efficiency, and providing a competitive edge.

Transformative Applications of AI in the Future

The continued development of AI technologies will lead to even more transformative applications in supply chain management, influencing key areas such as **forecasting**, inventory management, demand planning, logistics, and **supplier relationships**.

Predictive Analytics and Demand Forecasting

Predictive analytics powered by AI will continue to evolve, providing businesses with **more accurate forecasts** and **demand predictions**. AI's ability to analyze vast amounts of historical and real-time data allows for the identification of trends, seasonal patterns, and demand fluctuations with greater precision. This means supply chain managers will be able to better plan for future demand, improving inventory management, reducing stockouts or overstock situations, and aligning production schedules with consumer needs.

Real-Time Inventory Management

AI's role in **real-time inventory tracking and management** will be pivotal in improving supply chain efficiency. Through the use of IoT devices, sensors, and RFID technologies, supply chains will achieve greater visibility of inventory, enabling organizations to track products across the supply chain in real time. This data can be used by AI systems to optimize inventory levels, reduce waste, and streamline the replenishment process.

Autonomous Logistics and Transportation

One of the most exciting developments in AI for the supply chain is the use of **autonomous vehicles** and **drones** in logistics. AI-powered drones and autonomous trucks are set to revolutionize the transportation of goods. These technologies will reduce human intervention, optimize delivery routes, and enhance **supply chain speed** and **efficiency**.

Autonomous vehicles are expected to significantly reduce costs associated with labor, transportation, and fleet management.

Furthermore, the integration of **real-time route optimization** using AI will ensure deliveries are made in the most efficient way possible, reducing fuel consumption, transportation costs, and carbon emissions. **AI-powered fleets** will also increase the speed of last-mile deliveries, which are often one of the most expensive and time-consuming parts of the logistics process.

Intelligent Automation and Robotics

Automation has long been a key focus in manufacturing and warehousing, but the future will see **intelligent automation** powered by AI take center stage. In warehouses, **robotic process automation (RPA)**, **robotic picking**, and **sorting systems** will streamline processes, reducing the need for manual labor and enhancing operational efficiency. These robots will be capable of **learning from their environment** and improving their performance over time, making them more adaptable to changing conditions.

Moreover, AI will allow robots to collaborate seamlessly with humans in warehouses and factories, forming a **human-robot collaboration** model that will drive efficiency without sacrificing quality or flexibility.

AI-Driven Supply Chain Optimization

The use of AI for **supply chain optimization** is a rapidly growing area with tremendous future potential. By analyzing complex datasets from multiple sources, AI will enable companies to continuously optimize their supply chains in real time. This will allow businesses to improve decision-making, streamline operations, and enhance flexibility across the entire supply chain network.

In the future, AI will be able to optimize not only individual processes, such as procurement or distribution, but also the overall supply chain network. AI models will dynamically adjust production schedules, inventory levels, and delivery routes based on real-time demand and supply fluctuations, helping businesses become more responsive to market changes.

Advanced Scenario Planning

The future of AI in supply chain management will also involve **advanced scenario planning** tools that use AI to simulate different future outcomes based on various input parameters. This capability will allow businesses to assess potential risks, disruptions, and opportunities in the supply chain before they occur, enabling them to make better-informed decisions and develop more agile strategies.

AI-driven scenario planning tools will use **machine learning models** to simulate a wide range of possible events and their potential impacts on the supply chain. These tools will be able to consider various factors, such as **economic conditions**, **supply chain disruptions**, and **market changes**, to provide more accurate and actionable predictions.

Challenges and Ethical Considerations

While AI offers tremendous potential, its widespread adoption in supply chains is not without challenges. The **complexity** of AI systems, the **cost of implementation**, and the **need for skilled personnel** to manage these technologies may pose obstacles for some organizations, particularly smaller businesses.

Moreover, as AI becomes more embedded in supply chains, **ethical considerations** surrounding its use will need to be addressed. Ensuring that AI systems are **free from bias**, **transparent**, and **fair** will be essential for maintaining trust with stakeholders, customers, and employees. Companies must also consider the **impact on jobs** and workforces, as AI could displace certain manual roles, requiring significant investment in **upskilling** and **reskilling** initiatives.

AI in supply chains also raises **data privacy** and **security** concerns. As supply chains become more interconnected and data is shared across various partners, it becomes increasingly important to implement robust **cybersecurity** measures and ensure compliance with **data privacy regulations**.

The Role of AI in Sustainable Supply Chains

Sustainability will be a key theme for the future of AI in supply chain management. With increasing pressure on businesses to reduce their environmental impact, AI can play a crucial role in driving **sustainable practices**. By optimizing routes, improving energy efficiency in production, and reducing waste, AI will help businesses move toward more **eco-friendly** supply chains.

In addition, AI will enable more **precise tracking** of environmental metrics, allowing organizations to monitor their carbon footprint, track the sustainability of their suppliers, and make data-driven decisions to reduce waste and improve resource utilization. AI will also assist in creating more **circular supply chains** by enabling better product lifecycle management, reducing waste, and promoting recycling and reuse of materials.

Looking Ahead: AI and the Future of Supply Chain Management

As AI technologies continue to advance, the supply chain of the future will be more autonomous, intelligent, and resilient. AI's ability to handle complex data, predict outcomes, and optimize processes will make it an integral part of supply chain operations, enabling companies to respond faster to market demands and supply chain disruptions.

The future of AI in supply chain management is not just about automation; it is about creating smarter, more flexible supply chains that can adapt to changing market conditions, environmental pressures, and customer expectations. By embracing AI, organizations can unlock new levels of efficiency, sustainability, and competitive advantage, ultimately reshaping the way businesses operate and interact within the global supply chain ecosystem.

As AI continues to evolve, its potential to revolutionize supply chain management is boundless. The key to success will be for businesses to stay at the forefront of technological advancements, remain adaptable, and harness the power of AI to build more resilient, efficient, and sustainable supply chains for the future.

25. Call to Action for Leaders and Practitioners

As we stand at the precipice of a technological revolution in supply chain management, the call to action for leaders and practitioners is clear: embrace the potential of Artificial Intelligence (AI) to transform your supply chain operations. The era of data-driven decision-making, intelligent automation, and predictive insights is here, and those who act decisively today will shape the future of their businesses for years to come.

Understand the Strategic Importance of AI in Supply Chains

Leaders must recognize that AI is not just a technology investment, but a **strategic imperative**. The supply chain is the backbone of modern business operations, influencing everything from customer satisfaction to profitability. AI offers an opportunity to **optimize performance**, drive **efficiency**, and create new business models that were previously unimaginable. By adopting AI-driven technologies, companies can create a competitive edge that positions them for long-term success.

For practitioners, the first step in this journey is understanding the potential of AI for their specific roles and functions within the supply chain. Whether in procurement, logistics, inventory management, or demand forecasting, there is an AI application that can enhance the way you work. **Leverage AI as a tool to elevate your performance**, solve complex problems, and deliver value to your organization.

Invest in People: Training and Development are Key

A successful AI implementation in the supply chain requires more than just adopting new technologies; it requires a **change in mindset** and **cultural transformation**. Organizations must invest in their people by providing

training and **upskilling** opportunities to ensure that teams are ready to work alongside AI tools.

Leaders must make a commitment to continuous learning, providing access to resources that help employees develop the skills needed to operate, manage, and optimize AI systems. Creating an environment of **collaboration between AI systems and human expertise** is essential for realizing the full potential of AI technologies. Practitioners should actively pursue knowledge and **stay ahead of the curve** by exploring AI applications in their domain and adapting their approach to leverage these technologies for greater efficiency.

Foster a Culture of Innovation and Adaptability

AI is not a one-time project but an ongoing journey. The technologies driving the future of supply chain management are evolving at a rapid pace. To succeed in this environment, organizations must **foster a culture of innovation** and **continuous improvement**. Leaders should encourage experimentation, pilot projects, and the integration of AI into various facets of the supply chain. The willingness to **learn from failures**, **pivot**, and **adapt** to new insights is essential for long-term success.

Practitioners, too, must embrace a mindset of **adaptability**. AI will continue to evolve, and it's important to stay **open-minded** and **flexible** as new developments arise. Continuously evaluate the performance of AI applications and be proactive in exploring new use cases, technologies, and methodologies that can further enhance operations.

Collaborate with AI Experts and Partners

AI is a complex technology that requires a specialized understanding of data, algorithms, and system integration. As such, organizations should collaborate with AI experts, solution providers, and technology partners to ensure that their implementation strategy is sound and scalable. Leaders should actively seek partnerships with AI specialists who can guide them through the intricacies of deployment, from the selection of appropriate tools to the integration with existing systems.

Practitioners, on the other hand, should take the opportunity to **engage with AI professionals** and learn from their expertise. Collaborating with data scientists, machine learning engineers, and other AI experts will deepen your understanding of the technologies driving innovation and help you make more informed decisions in your day-to-day work.

Create a Data-Driven Organization

AI thrives on data, and the foundation of any AI-powered supply chain is a robust data infrastructure. Leaders must prioritize the development of a **data-driven culture** by ensuring that accurate, high-quality data is available and accessible across the organization. This includes investing in **data governance practices**, ensuring **data security**, and fostering **cross-functional collaboration** to eliminate silos.

For practitioners, it is crucial to **understand the role of data in AI systems**. Develop a mindset that values data collection, data accuracy, and continuous monitoring of data quality. By becoming more **data-literate**, practitioners can contribute to better AI outcomes and ensure that the insights generated by AI tools are based on accurate and relevant data.

Build a Roadmap for Scalable AI Adoption

The deployment of AI in the supply chain should not be an isolated project but a strategic, phased initiative that is aligned with long-term business goals. Leaders must create a clear roadmap for **AI adoption**, including short-term objectives, mid-term milestones, and long-term goals. This roadmap should outline key steps such as **pilot projects, proof of concept, scalability planning**, and **measuring success** through appropriate metrics.

Practical steps, such as identifying specific supply chain processes for initial AI application and ensuring the technology's scalability across functions and regions, are critical. Practitioners should participate in this process by identifying areas where AI can deliver the most immediate and tangible impact. Being part of these discussions will give you a sense of ownership and insight into the broader business strategy.

Ensure Ethical and Transparent AI Use

As AI becomes more integrated into the supply chain, the ethical considerations surrounding its use become more significant. Leaders must commit to ensuring that AI systems are **transparent, fair**, and **free from bias**. Ethical AI practices are not just a regulatory requirement but an important step toward building trust with customers, suppliers, and stakeholders. Creating **AI governance frameworks** and ensuring compliance with legal, regulatory, and ethical standards should be at the forefront of AI implementation.

For practitioners, understanding the ethical implications of AI in your work is equally important. **Advocate for transparency, data privacy**, and **bias mitigation** within your organization. Taking responsibility for ethical AI use will not only safeguard your company's reputation but also ensure the long-term success and acceptance of AI initiatives.

Drive Sustainability with AI

One of the most promising aspects of AI in supply chain management is its potential to drive **sustainability**. Leaders must recognize that AI technologies can be used to optimize resource use, reduce waste, enhance energy efficiency, and enable **greener** supply chains. In the future, sustainability will no longer be a luxury but a necessity, and AI will be a crucial enabler in achieving these goals.

For practitioners, there is an opportunity to **leverage AI for sustainable supply chain practices**, whether it's optimizing energy use in warehouses, reducing packaging waste, or improving demand forecasting to minimize unsold inventory. Sustainability is no longer just about compliance but about creating value and demonstrating social responsibility.

Lead the Change, Embrace the Future

The journey toward an AI-powered supply chain is an exciting one, filled with opportunities for innovation, efficiency, and growth. Leaders and practitioners alike must **embrace change**, stay curious, and be proactive in their pursuit of knowledge and improvement. AI is not just a tool for automation but a transformative force that will redefine how businesses operate in the coming decades.

As you move forward, remember that AI's potential in supply chain management is not limited to operational improvements—it can drive the **next generation of customer experiences**, enable **more sustainable** business practices, and open up entirely new business models. The future of supply chain management is AI-driven, and the time to act is now.

In conclusion, the call to action for leaders and practitioners is to **commit to a strategic, long-term vision** for AI integration, continuously **upskill and innovate**, and **lead**

with responsibility and **ethics** at the forefront. By doing so, you will not only enhance your organization's competitiveness but also contribute to a more sustainable, efficient, and intelligent global supply chain.

www.ingramcontent.com/pod-product-compliance
Lightning Source LLC
Chambersburg PA
CBHW052153220526
45471CB00004B/1657